Secrets

of

INSPIRATIONAL SELLING

How To
Inspire Your Customers to
Insist They Buy a Car from You

**For All Dealers,
Sales Managers,
& Salespeople**

by

D1026249

DAVID LEWIS

2008

SECRETS OF INSPIRATIONAL SELLING
Copyright 2008 by David Lewis

ISBN Number: 0-9646347-4-0

First Edition: January 2008
Current Printing: 9 8 7 6 5 4 3 2 1
Published in North America by David Lewis & Associates, Inc.
Printed in the United States of America
Book Design: Cricket Freeman, Possibilities Press
Cover Design: Cricket Freeman, Possibilities Press

CONTENTS

1
As You
Begin

The automobile industry has changed greatly since its infancy and the days of horseless carriages. Think about the industry back when a 1904 Cadillac had a single-cylinder 8 hp engine, was built one-by-one entirely by hand, and sold for a pricey $ 750. Now look at the industry today and consider:

> The advanced technology and design of vehicles.

> The modern marketing techniques to promote a variety of automobile models.

> The scientific repair and service of cars and trucks.

> The progressive management techniques to operate the dealerships.

Yes, cars and trucks – and the industry that sells them – have changed. But there is one thing that has always remained constant: The tremendous, basic desire people have to drive a shiny, new automobile. I don't think there is one person out there today who, under the right circumstances, would not like to be driving a new vehicle. So, with this strong, ever-present demand, why aren't we selling more cars? Why is the average Salesperson selling only eight to ten cars per month? Why aren't we reaching more buyers?

Let's look to the customer for answers. Buying a new car can be a nerve-racking experience. Not only do customers have to hopscotch their way through the selection process to find the car that's right for them, but once they decide to buy they have to worry about the deal they're getting:

> ➤ Are they buying a quality car?
> ➤ Are they paying too much?
> ➤ Can they trust the Dealer?

At the same time, buying a new car is one of the most thrilling times in their lives. This excitement is one of the elements that many of us, as automobile sales professionals, overlook and fail to take advantage of. We sell cars every day, so for us it's just another sale. But to them, it's a big day. Many people spend months – even years – saving to buy their new car, and will buy only one every four to six years. You must remember that for most buyers this is the second largest investment they will make, after the purchase of a home. And for many who have not bought a home, it is the largest.

We need to take a closer look at how we approach these customers to sell cars. Even though we all agree the industry has changed, the basic want and need of the buyer has not. But the way they shop, compare, and buy *has* changed.

In choosing a vehicle, the buyer of today has so many choices, both as to make and model. The customer can select from sedans, coupes, hatchbacks, two-doors, four-doors, convertibles, minivans, minitrucks, full-size vans, full-size trucks, utility vehicles, and more.

Then consider how many different dealerships there are in any given market area. In many communities customers can have five or more dealerships selling the same product within ten miles of their home. Think how many more would be available to them if they were to consider a different make or going only a little further away from home to buy.

How do you get them to choose you over all those others?

Yes, there is a lot of competition from other dealerships. But you can take an unusual approach. You can make yourself unique in the buyers' eyes, someone they are not only willing to do business with, but *insist* upon.

Now take into consideration the competitive advertising, the How-To-Buy-A-Car guide books, and the information provided by television. And let's not forget the newest source of data for new car buyers: the Internet. All of that adds up to an overwhelming avalanche of information. Sometimes I think it's amazing that customers don't get more confused than they presently are.

But that's only part of the details customers have to deal with in order to make a decision. They include:
- ➢ Whether to lease or buy.
- ➢ If leasing, which plan is the most favorable for their circumstances.
- ➢ If buying, whether to finance or pay cash.
- ➢ If financing, where to finance:
  - ○ The dealership's Finance Department.
  - ○ Credit union.
  - ○ Local bank.

Unquestionably, all this information has led to a better informed buyer. And a more knowledgeable buyer has necessitated a shift in how cars are sold. Therefore, if you want to attract the majority of buyers, how you address your customers and their needs must shift also. You need to motivate your customers. Not just influence them, but to *INSPIRE* them to insist they buy from you. If you can do that you can mold a successful place for yourself in the industry.

Selling cars today has become a superb profession, ripe with opportunities. The industry has had so many exciting changes over the last ten years, creating many possibilities for success. For instance, Dealers today manage and operate businesses that produce millions of dollars a year in revenue, yet come from all ethnic and economic backgrounds and many have very little formal education. The diversity of our national workforce reflects that variety in our customers, which cannot be said of many other industries.

Also the chance for advancement is stronger in the automobile business than any other industry. Of the 5,000 or more individuals who will enter into an automobile sales career this year:

> 35% of them will become Sales Managers within five years.
> 10% of them will become General Managers within ten years.
> About 1% to 3% will become Dealers within twenty years.

There are few other industries which offer such a great opportunity for advancement.

Of course, there are numerous factors that are going to influence each individual's success in this dynamic industry. Some of those might be the economic times, the Dealer's support, being in the right place at the right time, or just plain luck. But the greatest opportunity will come to those who have the determination, drive, and desire for success.

If you are an individual who can put forth your best effort to truly learn, to be passionate about your career, to care seriously about your customers as well as yourself, you can grow with the industry.

Success can come to anyone who wants to be successful.

The one controllable aspect of your future is you! You hold the key to success. Some of you are content selling cars and some of you have dreams of one day becoming Sales Manager, or even owning a dealership. Whatever your dreams are, if you stay focused on that dream it will come true.

This book was written with one goal: To provide Salespeople, Sales Managers, General Managers, and Dealers such as you with a strategy to achieve your own goals.

I believe all of you want to sell more cars and make more money. The way to do that is to have a unique sales technique. The concept of *INSPIRATIONAL SELLING* may not be new to our industry, but the system in this book provides a new perspective for how to *INSPIRE* people to insist they buy from you.

In reading this book, keep an open mind. Be objective as you encounter these fresh ideas, even if you might not initially agree with them. I have seen them double the number of cars a Salesperson sold each month.

Good Luck and Enjoy!

By the way, I suggest that to fully absorb this approach to selling you should read this book a number of times. It is amazing how many additional ideas you will pick up the second or third time you read through it.

✦

2
The Mercedes
Benz Story

A number or years ago my wife and I decided it was time for us to purchase a new car. Like everyone else, we had to go car shopping. But surprisingly we found we weren't really looking forward to the process. We knew it would be trying. We assessed our position: As a trade-in we had a seven-year-old Audi that my wife had been driving since it was new. We were willing to put down an additional $ 2,000 in cash and we had established a budget of around $450 per month.

Our first step was to determine what kind of vehicle we wanted to buy. So for the next couple of weeks we went to all kinds of dealerships, looking at all kinds of cars, hoping to find one we liked. But no luck.

As we were leaving every dealership, each Salesperson would make the same comments: "Now don't forget," they'd tell us, "We have the best dealership in town and we will give you the best price." The one comment both of us always got a kick out of was: "Go get your best price, bring it to us, and we'll beat it by $100."

My wife would turn to me and say, "Why don't they just give us their best price now?"

The ironic thing was that in this part of our shopping process we really weren't looking for the best price. We were just looking to find a car we liked. Once we found that car, then we would worry about the price.

We looked at four-door sedans, coupes, convertibles. We even considered a utility vehicle. And even though I knew a Mercedes Benz was well out of our price range I'd always wanted to own one. So at the end of every day we'd spent looking at cars I would comment to my wife, "Honey, let's go look at a Mercedes Benz next time."

One Saturday morning with nothing on our schedules, once again I said to my wife, "Hey, let's go look at a Mercedes."

And that's exactly what we did. We got up, showered, threw on some clothes, and drove over to the local Mercedes Benz dealership. Now, understand, on a Saturday I often look like a grub: unshaven, in sweat pants and a sweatshirt. I'm sure I looked like the last thing a Mercedes Benz Salesperson wanted to see walking into the dealership door to shop their line of cars that Saturday morning. But, what did it matter to us? We were just looking.

On our way over to the dealership I reminded my wife of the standard three lies that we were telling every Salesperson. I'd say, "Don't forget: We're paying cash, we're not buying a car today, and the Audi is worth $6,000." But I knew all three of those comments weren't true because we couldn't afford to pay cash, we would buy a car that day if someone was strong enough to sell it to us, and our Audi was only worth about $2,200 ACV.

So, why would we want to lie by telling the Salesperson these three things?

Because, obviously, we wanted the best deal. We felt if we were paying cash and weren't buying that day, they'd give us a lowball number to begin negotiations. Also, if we told them our car was worth more, they'd give us more for the trade.

As we arrived at this Mercedes Benz dealership we got out of our car and the Salesperson came out, introduced himself to us, and welcomed us to the dealership. He then told us his name and shook our hands, just like they had at every other dealership.

But from that point forward, we were astonished at how professionally we were treated. Even considering the way we were dressed, the way we looked, and the car we were driving, this individual insisted on calling us Mr. and Mrs. Lewis. And you know what? It made me feel good. It made my wife feel important. And we liked that.

Now, at this point, most Salespeople would start the pre-qualifying questions:

- "What are you looking for?"
- "What size?"
- "What is your budget?"
- "Where do you work?
- "Are you paying cash or financing?"

To most people, including ourselves, those questions are very threatening. And in many cases, because we had been put on the defensive, we lied about the answers.

But at the Mercedes Benz dealership the Salesperson's questions were different. He asked:

➢ "What are you looking for in a vehicle?"

> ➤ "What standard features are most important to you?"
> ➤ "What extra options would you like?"

Without hesitation we answered very sincerely and honestly, "We're looking for a mid-size four-door sedan, with basic options."

He had a very positive response to our needs, and then invited us to join him on the lot to see what they had available.

What he did next I found extremely interesting. Because, remember, he never tried to pre-qualify us based on budget or size. He walked us over to the first row of vehicles and showed us the most inexpensive, basic four-door sedan: the 190E.

What I did immediately was what most buyers do: I walked over and I looked at the window sticker. The car was about $29,000. I did not flinch. I walked around and we both continued looking at the car. You see, what we did was to send that Salesperson a signal: We could afford the vehicle and initially liked it.

He didn't have to pre-qualify us. If he had, we would probably have lied to him. If he had asked us what our budget was we would have told him that it was lower than what we could actually spend. Thinking a new car was out of our budget, he would have taken us to the used car department, wasting his time and ours since we were not in the market for a used car.

His next step was to ask us, "Would you like to sit inside the car? See if it fits your needs?"

We said, "Sure."

He went into the dealership, came right back out with the keys. He jumped in the driver's seat, started up the car, put it in drive, pulled it out, opened the doors, and my wife and I jumped in and shut the doors.

Within fifteen seconds we knew this car wasn't for us. We felt cramped and tight, the doors felt flimsy. We didn't like it and we made that clear to the Salesperson immediately.

He said, "No problem." He backed it back into the space. "Let me move you up to the next line of cars."

We then went and looked at the Mercedes 300E. And, of course, the first thing I did was to walk over to the window sticker, which was $ 44,410. I made a small comment about the price but we kept looking at the car. Again, sending the Salesperson a signal: We could afford the car.

In actuality, weighing the budget we'd determined beforehand for the purchase of a new car, we knew we couldn't afford that car. But that didn't stop us.

We walked around it, we looked in it.

He suggested, "Why don't I get the keys and you can sit inside this one?" He went inside, came right back out, started it up, pulled it out, and opened up both doors.

We jumped in the car, shut the doors, and we could tell right off the bat we loved it. The doors felt strong and sturdy, the big windshield gave us a beautiful panoramic view, it was a fine vehicle.

The Salesperson could see it, too. It showed. My wife was sitting behind the steering wheel, touching everything. I was nodding.

The Salesperson got in the backseat. He then started to go over the interior parts of the car, almost as though he was doing the physical delivery. He showed my wife how the radio and CD player worked. He showed her how to operate the air-conditioner, the heater, the rear window defogger, how to adjust the mirrors and how to open and close the windows. He spent ten minutes going over everything with her.

Then he asked us, "Would you like to take a ride in the car?"

Of course we said, "Yes."

As my wife was starting to pull out of the dealership she asked him, "Where do you want me to go?" She felt she had to ask because at every other dealership the Salesperson was very clear about what route to take on a test drive.

But once again, this Salesperson was different. He replied by asking her, "Are you familiar with the area?"

My wife answered, "Oh, yeah. We don't live far away."

He then told her, "Drive the car wherever you'd like to go."

This type of salesmanship was so refreshing. In most dealerships we visited we were never treated this well. At most, after being pre-qualified, the Salesperson would tell us what we could afford, what we could buy, and the test drive consisted of "Turn right, now turn left, O.K., let's switch drivers," and then directly back to the dealership. The longest test drive we had taken up until this point was about ten minutes.

Even though the test drives were short, the Salespeople spent the entire time quizzing us. They'd ask us:

- "How does it feel?
- "How does it drive?"
- "How's your visibility?"
- "Isn't this a great car?"

But you know, one of those things I told my wife prior to arriving at each dealership was to never show too much excitement about any particular car. So after each question she was very good at giving basic, noncommittal responses.

However, this test drive in the Mercedes 300E was definitely different than the others. No other Salesperson had gone over the car as well as he did here, treated us so kindly – and more importantly – made us feel so comfortable with the sales process. During the entire test drive he sat in the backseat of the car and never said a word.

You know what?

My wife and I talked. I ended up asking my wife the obvious questions:

- "How does it ride?"
- "How does it feel?"
- "How's its maneuverability?"

➢ "How's your view?"

For fifteen to twenty minutes we talked and he sat back there and listened.

Finally my wife asked him, "Do we need to go back now?"

He said, "Nope. Whenever you're ready is fine with me."

He knew the longer we drove this car, the more we'd fall in love with it.

Eventually we switched drivers and I drove the rest of the way back to the dealership. When we pulled in he never gave us any of those sales gimmick lines like, "Park it in the sold line. That way nobody else will look at the car while we negotiate price."

Refreshingly he said, "Pull in wherever you want to park, wherever it's convenient."

I pulled it in, parked it, turned it off, and we all got out of the car.

He then started to do his walk-around presentation on the exterior of the vehicle. This was the most impressive walk-around I had ever been exposed to in my life. Sure, he went through all the features that were basic on the car. He opened the trunk and the hood, and showed us all the technology. In almost every dealership we had visited the Salesperson pointed out fuel injection. So did this Mercedes Salesperson. But he went one step further. He asked, "How familiar are you with how the fuel injection system works?"

To which my wife responded by saying, "Not at all."

So you know what he did?

He explained it in detail, using terminology that was very easy for her to understand. He asked her, "Do you remember years ago how when you used to start a car you had to pump the pedal a number of times? And if you did it too much you might flood the carburetor?"

Her response was just what he expected. She did remember doing that.

"Well," he explained to her, "With the technology of the fuel injection system, when you turn the key to start the car a computer now tells it how much fuel to send in so the car will start every time without hesitation."

My wife found this very interesting. And she was now even more impressed with this Salesperson.

But he did not stop there. He spent about twenty minutes explaining how all the new features worked: From how the ABS brakes stopped the car to how the airbag system functioned.

Next came another question we had not been exposed to before. He asked us, "How important is the safety of the vehicle in your buying decision?"

My wife said, "Oh, very important." You see, my wife had been involved in a serious accident a number of years earlier and since that time had been very concerned about the safety features of automobiles.

He said, "Then let me share with you some of the things about the Mercedes Benz that makes it one of the safest vehicles on the road. First of all, Mercedes Benz studies the rate of injuries in automobile accidents. They found one of the most frequent types of injuries occurs from the shattering of glass. So what they've done is to install glass that does not shatter. This way, if you're involved in an accident and the windshield breaks, that glass will not shatter. It will stay within its own frame."

My wife thought that was the neatest thing in the world.

But you know what was very interesting? (And I knew this.) Every car sold in the United States, after a certain date, must have that feature. It is called tempered glass.

But my wife did not know that. She believed it was unique to Mercedes. And the reason she came to that conclusion was because no other Salesperson had taken the time to explain it.

The Salesperson then explained that under the hood there were these bars that would collapse the hood in case of a head-on collision. He said that they'd found through studies that a lot of times when people were injured it was because in a front-end collision the hood entered the vehicle. He explained that this hood folded like an accordion so that it wouldn't come into the car.

Again, my wife was very impressed. But again, she didn't know it was standard equipment and required by law.

He explained how there were sidebeams in the doors so if the car was hit broadside she would be better protected.

And again, every car has to have reinforced sidebeams. However, my wife thought that all of these safety features were only available on a Mercedes Benz.

The best part of all came when he again mentioned the options of airbags and ABS brakes. He sounded so nonchalant as he said, "Oh, and by the way, like all other cars, we have airbags and ABS brakes as well."

My wife was buying into this hook, line, and sinker.

And the funny thing was: So was I.

We had now been with this Salesperson for about an hour and a half and we were truly enjoying our experience. He took his time, was very caring, and more importantly, he knew his product very well and gave us information that nobody else did.

We had now come to the part of the presentation when most Salespeople would go for their main trial close. And so did he. But his was different. He asked us, "Does this vehicle meet the standards and qualities you're looking for?"

How in the world could we have said "No."?

Compare that to what most other Salespeople had said to us: "If we could come together on terms and numbers, are you ready to buy a car today?"

You know what my wife and I would always say?

"Nope." The best part about that answer was watching the expression on the Salesperson's face. Most got a look of total rejection and discouragement.

If we said "No," then they would ask us the stupidest questions. Like:

- "How come?"
- "Why not?"
- "Would you like to look at other cars?"

Discouraged, they'd say, "Obviously, you haven't found a car you like."

After this minor setback for the Salesperson, my wife and I knew we were in a stronger position to negotiate. We'd sit down at their desk and each Salesperson would up and leave for the Sales Manager's desk or podium, only to come back with a lowball price or a statement such as: "Go do all your shopping. When you get your best price, come back in and my Manager said that we'll beat it."

What a way to sell a car!

Now remember, this particular Salesperson at the Mercedes Benz dealership did not ask us if we were ready to buy a car today. Because if he had, we would have told him the same thing we'd told everyone else: "No."

Instead, he asked us if this vehicle met the qualities and standards we were looking for in transportation. We had no alternative but to say "Yes," because it did.

He then said, "Come on, I'd like to show you something very unique about our dealership. I think you'll find it interesting." He walked us into his service center, and here is where the true salesmanship came out. Keep in mind that only half the people in the other dealerships bothered to even show us their service center. And when they did, it was a two-minute presentation, at best.

This Salesperson walked us in and started telling us how important service was to this dealership, that they were going to go far beyond the call of duty to take care of our service needs, and that he wanted to share with us some unique things about his service center. He explained how it was organized with specialties, like doctors. Just as when you have a problem with your ears, you go to an ear, nose, and throat specialist; a problem with your eyes, you go to an ophthalmologist; or a problem with allergies, you go to an allergist. It was the same here at the dealership. He showed us how each service tech was a specialist in their area: This service tech only handled transmissions, this one engine work, this one electrical, this one did lube, filter, and tune-ups. By developing their service center like this we would be getting specialized attention for any repair needed.

Once again, this setup is very common in automobile dealerships. But my wife didn't know that because no one else took the time to describe how their Service Departments operated.

He then explained to us how they had just invested in this new piece of equipment. You know what it was? It was the Sun diagnostic machine which, of course, I'd seen before. It did look fairly new, but it's a very old type of technology. He detailed that all they had to do when we had a mechanical failure was hook this machine up and within a matter of minutes it would spit out a report telling the technician what was wrong. This way, if we ever had a breakdown, they could save us lots of money on diagnosing the problem.

Once again, my wife was fascinated because she had never seen this type of equipment before and he had introduced her to it.

He then walked us over to his Parts Department and told us they inventoried over $ 200,000 worth of Mercedes parts. With that many parts at their disposal, if our vehicle did break down, there wouldn't be a delay in repairing the car.

My wife thought this was great.

But you know what? $ 200,000 in parts is not a lot. Most dealerships inventory over half a million dollars in parts. But like many people, she did not know that.

What happened next was by far the most impressive piece of salesmanship I'd seen. He walked us over to the service counter where the Service Manager was catching up on some paperwork. The Salesperson introduced us to him and told him we were considering purchasing a brand new Mercedes 300E.

The Service Manager stuck out his hand, shook our hands, and said, "Oh, you folks must be very excited. That's a wonderful automobile."

And my wife said, "Yes, we are!" – just as though we'd already made a decision to buy the car.

The Service Manager said, "I'm sure that John has gone over our Service Department in great detail. But let me take a few minutes more and tell you a few extra things." He explained to us what the service hours were, that they had night hours two days a week, that they did lube, oil, and filters every morning from 7:00 to 9:00, and that they could do them in thirty minutes or less, just like the jiffy and quick lubes. He shared with us that they had a free shuttle service every morning and afternoon. Then he asked us who would be responsible for the maintenance on the vehicle.

I pointed to my wife and said, "Well, it's going to be her car."

He replied, "Good." Turning to my wife he added, "Mrs. Lewis, there are a couple of things you must keep in mind. Number one: In the first thirty to sixty days of driving, your car might burn a quick quart of oil. So continually check the oil and don't be concerned if it's down a quart. Number two: We highly recommend lube, oil, and filters every ninety days or 3,000 miles." He told us if we did that on a consistent basis we would always have a well-running automobile. Then he said, "That means your first oil change will be due on..." and he actually gave us a specific date three months later.

I thought my wife was going to take out her calendar and write down to bring in the car for service on that particular date.

Not only had the Salesperson and his Service Manager successfully sold the benefits of the vehicle, but they were very convincing at selling the benefits of the dealership, and obviously, if we were buying the car and the dealership, that must mean we really liked the Salesperson, too.

The Service Manager then extended his hand, shook our hands one more time, congratulated us, and wished us the best of luck with our new car.

You know what my wife said?

"Oh, thank you. And I'll see you in ninety days."

And he said, "Wonderful, and don't forget."

I couldn't believe what was happening.

Walking back into the dealership the Salesperson invited us to come sit down at his desk, saying, "I'd like to get some more information." He pulled out a worksheet.

Would you believe it? We never hesitated once to answer any of his questions. We gladly gave him our address and phone number. I even gave him my business number and email address.

Why? Because he had built up a level of rapport and trust with us – rapport at its best level. He never pressured us; we felt very comfortable.

He then came out with, "Folks, I'm sure at this time you'd be very excited to find out what your investment will be in this automobile."

And obviously, we said, "Yes."

He picked up the telephone, called somebody, (who I assumed was the Sales Manager) and said, "Could I please have the investment on stock number 802? It's a silver Mercedes 300E." A few seconds later he spoke into the phone, "Uh-huh, uh-huh, uh-huh." while making notes, then hung up. He told us we could purchase the vehicle with $4,441 down and our monthly investment would be $700 a month for sixty months. He twisted the piece of paper toward us and came right out and said, "Folks, would you like to purchase the vehicle?"

My wife turned to me and said, "We can afford that."

I could not believe my ears. How many times had I told her not to show any emotions about how much we liked a particular car?

But the hard part was I agreed with her. I loved the car. I felt the dealership had a lot to offer and I was truly enjoying our buying experience.

And then something clicked with me. I held up my hand. "Wait a minute. Let's slow this process down. We forgot to tell you we have a trade-in."

He said, "Oh, fantastic. Let me get some information on your trade."

What a different approach. Everyone else wanted to know what our trade-in was before they even did a demonstration ride. They even wanted know what we thought our car was worth. He didn't want to know any of that. He was not interested in whether we had a trade-in up until this point because selling his dealership, selling his car, and selling himself has absolutely nothing to do with whether we had a trade-in or not.

He filled out an appraisal slip then had a Manager go out and appraise our car. A few minutes later he came back. He proposed a new number: with the $ 4,441 down, our monthly investment would now be $ 610 a month, including our trade-in. Then he asked us again, "Would you like to purchase the vehicle?"

Again, my wife jumped in and said, "We can afford that."

Now at this point in time I already knew we were going to buy the car. So, being in the automobile business I said, "Hey, I love it. I love what you're doing, but I need you to do me a favor. I'd like to know the invoice on the car, I'd like to know the ACV on the trade-in, and I'd like to know for how much over "invoice" you're going to sell us the car." Then I gave him my business card and I said, "Look, I'm in the business."

His response to me was, "Oh, I know you're in the business. I know exactly who you are. I've seen you on ASTN, listened to your tapes, watched your videos, and I've seen your ad in *The Automotive News.*"

You want to know what was really neat about that? I had been at other dealerships where they had recognized me. I actually had two situations where people came over to me and asked, "Are you just stroking us? We know who you are."

And both times I said, "No. I need to buy a car, just like everybody else."

This particular Salesperson at the Mercedes Benz dealership didn't care who I was. He knew his job was to sell his dealership, sell his product, and sell himself.

After a quick phone call the Sales Manager came over and introduced himself to us. I restated what I wanted to know about the invoice amount, trade-in ACV, and the amount over "invoice" that they needed to charge us. He left and returned a few minutes later and said, "Here's the information." He showed us the invoice, told us the ACV on our car was $2,200, and that they needed to make $2,000 on the vehicle. He told us our new monthly investment for sixty months was now $560.

I then asked, "What would our monthly investment be for thirty-six months?"

He came back and gave it to us.

I turned to my wife. "Honey, do you like the car?"

She smiled and said, "I love it."

I asked her, "Would you like to buy it?"

Her smile broadening, she said, "Yes."

I turned to the Sales Manager and the Salesperson. "You've got a deal."

And guess what? We drove home that day with a brand new Mercedes 300E.

Why?

Because we were sold it – even though the car was out of our price range.

As we pulled away from the dealership in our new car, my wife turned to me and said, "I'm happy, but I'm confused. You told me we weren't buying a car today, we were paying cash, and our car was worth $6,000."

I patted her shoulder. "Ah, Honey, don't worry about it. That's what I wanted you to think, because that's what I wanted you to say. Don't worry, we got a great deal."

You know what the real kick was?

I found out later that at $2,000 they made a heck of a gross on us.

But we didn't care. I had other people tell me I could have bought that car for as little as $500 over invoice. We didn't care – because we liked the dealership, we loved the car, and we truly appreciated the way the Salesperson handled us.

You see, the difference is this: They sold us, where other people ignored us, pressured us, and told us. I don't believe we received this *INSPIRING* sales presentation just because we were in a Mercedes dealership. It could have been any type of dealership selling any type of vehicles. What's important is the type of presentation we received.

Now after hearing this story I ask you: Why should I buy a car from you when I can buy it for the same price, or less, somewhere else?

The reason has got to be because:
  ➤ You're going to be unique and show me why.
  ➤ You're going to sell me the value of your dealership better than anybody else does.
  ➤ You're going to sell me the value of your product better than anybody else does.
  ➤ And you're going to make a better impression on me than anybody else does.

That would *INSPIRE* me to buy the car from you.

Even if you were $ 200 higher than the dealership down the street, I would probably still buy it from you. Because you take the time, never hurry me or hustle me, and show me you care. You never put me on the defensive, never place me in a position where I feel I need to lie. And you listen and are sensitive to my needs. You know your product well and share your knowledge easily. You encourage the excitement of buying a new car. By inspiring me, you build a bond between us.

Selling is creating that bond – that much-sought-after trust between buyer and Salesperson. Do it well and you will be very, very successful.

3
Understanding
the Customer

You're a new Salesperson, or perhaps you've been selling cars for years. Either way, to increase your sales you must look closely at customers: Who you think they are and who they really are. Before you can begin the sales process you must first analyze and understand your customers. Among other things you need to know:

> What they think of the existing selling processes.
> What makes them buy.
> What keeps them from buying.
> Why they choose one dealership over another.

The customer of today is very different from the customer of years ago. Today we are in a buyer's market where the buyer has all the factors stacked in their favor. They have a huge variety of products from which to choose, numerous dealerships within a short drive, and tremendous resources for information. Think about it: Today a buyer can access any number of web sites on the Internet and get the answers to almost any conceivable question, including current vehicle costs, rebates, and dealership incentives. For a small fee they can receive a print out of this information, plus a list of dealerships in their local area that will sell them the car for cost, or perhaps even below cost.

As proof of this highly competitive buyer's market just take a look at how dealerships are hustling to attract customers. They've even launched an aggressive advertising "civil war" amongst themselves, doing whatever it takes in their advertising to get the customer in the door. They're offering money-back guarantees on their cars, prices below invoice, and promotions ensuring bank approval. However, in this "civil war" the only true winner is the customer.

Believe it or not, most customers today are savvy enough to realize they're in a buyer's market. They've learned how to maneuver through the game to get the best price, learning the best serves, volleys, backhands, and returns. And there is nothing wrong with that. They didn't create the game, the automobile industry did.

You know, when every four years or so I become a new car buyer I, too, want the best product at the best price. So I, too, play the game. Don't you?

Now, how do you think most Salespeople look at today's market and today's customers? Any differently than they did ten, five, or even two years ago?

Let me take a minute to tell you a little story about rats, cheese, and automobile Salespeople. If you put a rat in front of a bunch of tunnels and put cheese at the end of one of them, the rat will run up and down each tunnel striving for the cheese. If you do this repeatedly and always put the cheese at the end of the fourth tunnel, eventually the rat will learn and go down the fourth tunnel first, and successfully chew on his cheese. However, if you're tricky and then put the cheese at the end of any other tunnel, the rat will still go down the fourth tunnel ready for his cheese. When it's not there he'll come out perplexed, look around, and run right back down the fourth tunnel to no cheese! He's following a simple rule: If it worked once, it should always work.

Sound like any Salespeople you know?

Now, the difference between rats and people is that, given enough time, rats will stop going down the fourth tunnel and try a new one. But human beings care more about going down the right tunnel, even when their senses tell them it isn't producing results. Humans keep doing what they do, despite a lack of rewards, because they believe what they are doing is what is correct. And they will continue to do it, even if there is never cheese in their tunnel again, as long as they believe what they're doing is right.

But you're not like other Salespeople. Learn from the rat, try a new tunnel. Try a new method of selling.

The market has changed, the buyer has changed. Customers today shun aggressive Salespeople with their overly friendly behavior, demanding demeanor, repeat phone calls, questioning attitude, or anything that can be perceived as high pressure. And yet, many Salespeople hang on to ideas about customers that have been passed on from Salesperson to Salesperson over the years with no real explanation. But they have become outdated myths.

Let's weigh some of the most common ones.

MYTH #1:

Each car buyer is different in their own way.

Many Salespeople will tell you import buyers are different from domestic buyers. Salespeople of high line cars believe their customers are different from the customers who buy less expensive cars. And some feel those who pay cash are different than those who finance.

What, then, would make one customer different from another? Their social, economic, or financial background?

I don't think so.

You might even say they are as different from one another as the cars they drive.

But are they? Let's just say that you and I are sitting in my car outside a relative's home. In the garage is a brand new Volvo. Now, what conclusions could you make about this couple as car buyers, based on their car?

Well, you might say they're probably middle-aged people, financially secure, and safety-minded. You might add they're most likely solid shoppers who read all the consumer magazines and books.

Now, as we're sitting in my car analyzing the type of buyers they are, the husband pulls into the driveway in his four-year-old, Chevrolet, S-10 pick-up truck. He parks it right next to the wife's Volvo. As he gets out you see a man in his mid-60's, dressed in dirty jeans, flannel shirt, and sneakers. Now what type of people and buyers are they?

A little confused now? You see, this couple, my parents, are what I consider typical car buyers: They're hard-working people who happen to enjoy the luxury of a full-size import sedan, but at the same time enjoy the ruggedness of a truck. In shopping for both cars they followed the same procedures and thought process for each purchase. They wanted to buy a quality vehicle from a Salesperson and dealership that they liked, they wanted to be treated courteously, and of course, they wanted a great deal. So again, what type of buyers are my parents? They're typical car buyers!

So, is each car buyer different in their own way?

No, it is a myth. When it comes right down to it: A buyer is a buyer is a buyer. All buyers want:

> To be treated with respect.
> To have a knowledgeable, courteous Salesperson guide them through the sales process.
> To receive a good price on a quality product.

MYTH #2:

Customers want to lie to get the best deal.

I've always been told: Buyers are liars. But I never realized they deliberately lied until, as a Salesperson who was now a buyer, I entered a dealership and told my wife, "Now, don't forget, we're not buying a car today, our trade is worth X amount of dollars, and, if asked, we're paying cash." I had just become one of them, a buyer who lies. As we visited other dealerships I was amazed at how easy the lying became. If a Salesperson asked me what prices we'd received at other dealerships we'd visited, I could lie in a heartbeat. I'm not a believer in lying, but it did not take long for me to justify the lying in my own mind. We lied for the same reasons all customers lie: To get the best deal.

The ironic thing was I realized the lying was actually hurting, not helping. For example, one of the numerous lies I told pertained to our budget. I discovered that because of the lie Salespeople were showing us cars we didn't like, cars that were smaller, with less options. The reason the cars didn't suit became obvious: We lied! We could afford more and knew it. But the Salespeople did not. They were only showing us cars that fit the budget we said we could afford.

Just like all customers, we didn't lie because we wanted to, but because we thought it would get us a good deal. But customers won't lie if they feel they don't have to.

So how do you stop your customers from lying?

It's really quite simple: Stop asking questions that will cause customers to lie, such as:

- What is your budget?
- What do you think your trade is worth?
- What kind of deal have you found at other dealerships?

MYTH #3:

You have to lie to make the deal.

So, the customer doesn't lie just because they want to lie. They often lie because they feel pressured and need a way out of the dealership. And they lie because they believe you will lie to them just to get the sale. With all this distrust, it's amazing any sales are ever concluded.

Show your customers your professionalism and integrity:

➢ Convey only the truth.
➢ Stand behind what you say.

MYTH #4:

You have to ask the customer certain questions to qualify them.

Many Salespeople want to find out as fast as possible whether customers are paying cash or financing. Some wouldn't dream of taking customers for a demo ride until they've totally qualified them by asking their budget so they can show them the right car. There are those that want to know right away if they have a trade and if so, what the customers think it's worth. And then there are the Salespeople who can't commit themselves on anything until they know what kind of deal customers can get elsewhere.

But I'd like for you to take a minute and truly ask yourself, "Do I really need to know this?"

Remember: The sale is made when just three factors fall into place:

➤ The customers like the product.
➤ They like the dealership.
➤ And they like you.

Any other information is superfluous, and could be considered offensive by the customer if you ask for it. Think about it: Knowing what they want for their trade or what kind of deal they can get elsewhere has nothing to do with whether or not they like the car, the dealership, or you. As you will discover in other chapters, you don't even need to know their budget to effectively sell them a car.

MYTH #5:

Customers can't make up their minds, so you have to do it for them.

Recently when my wife and I purchased a new family vehicle we were staggered by the number of questions thrust at us. I can't tell you how difficult the Salespeople made it for us. We probably visited four or five dealerships (I lost count because so many of them treated us the same way that they're all running together in my mind).

Contrary to what these Salespeople thought, it wasn't hard for us to find a car we liked. What made it difficult was weeding through their perplexing presentations to determine the price we would pay and if we liked the dealership enough to purchase the car there.

One way you can make yourself and your dealership unique is to listen, to hear the customer's needs, to develop the ability to put yourself in the customer's shoes. They will make up their minds based on sound information you have given them as a response to what they have told you.

MYTH #6:

Once a customer goes out the door, you've lost them.

Lookers are not buyers. As Salespeople, we often get upset when customers say they are "Just looking!" or leave our dealership to go and shop. When I was in the retail end of the business I, like most of you, got caught up in the notion that buying a car was easy and could be done in sixty minutes (or less). I didn't understand why many customers looked and then left.

Buyers today are concerned with price, but also with reliability of the product and with whom they do business. Studies show approximately 70% of the people that visit your dealership will buy a car within ten to fourteen days. Buyers today like to take their time; they're choosier. Shopping is now a common denominator for all buyers and you can't change that fact. Let them shop.

MYTH #7:

To customers, price is the most important factor.

Many of you think price is critical, that customers will sell you out to the dealership down the street for $50. Sometimes that is true, some do, but not for the reason you think.

It is not because price is the most important factor to them, but because you made it the issue. Why do people in the automobile industry feel compelled to do that? Everyday in every industry people pay more to do business with people they've chosen based on factors other than price, whether it be their doctor, lawyer, tailor, or hairstylist. They buy from people they trust, have treated them well, and they like. But remember: (and I will continually repeat this phrase throughout the book) If all things are equal, then price is the only factor.

So, to keep price from being the factor of lone importance, you must make yourself and your dealership a unique factor. That is why you must *INSPIRE* the customer.

The customer is it. They're the reason we go to work everyday. Without them we have nothing. The better you understand your customer, the way they think, view the sales process, and want to be treated, the stronger a Salesperson you will become.

4

**Inspiring
Your Customers
to Buy from You**

The first time I visit a dealership as a trainer and get together with the Salespeople and Sales Managers I always start the conversation by asking all of them this question: "If I shop three dealerships, why should I buy the car from you?"

Each time all the responses are virtually the same. I'd be willing to bet your answer to that question is one of them.

They respond with:
- "We have a great selection."
- "We have a great Service Department."
- "We have better Salespeople."
- "We have a great facility."
- And so on.

But they always conclude with: "We will give you the best price."

To which I ask, "What if I was given the same price at all three dealerships?" And again I ask them, "Why should I buy the car from you?"

And again I get the same answers. Plus a few blank looks as if to say, "What else is there to say?"

So here comes the twist. What if – and this is highly possible – that at each dealership they all stated the same things: They have a great selection, great service, great facility, great Salespeople, and a great price. So why should I buy the car from you? What becomes the deciding factor if all these things are equal?

This is the point when customers are left with no alternative but to make price the determining factor. So if one dealership beats the others' prices by only $50, then that dealership will make the sale.

However, you can create an atmosphere where price is not the main deciding factor, and that is through the concept of *INSPIRATIONAL SELLING.*

Now, do not misunderstand my thoughts, if you are $500 or more higher than the competition, then price, naturally, would make a difference. Nobody is going to pay a whole lot more just because you did a great job. But, customers will pay an additional $100,

$200, $300, or maybe even $400, because they want to do business with you.

And you can *INSPIRE* them to want to do business with you through *INSPIRATIONAL SELLING*.

How? By telling them how great you and your dealership are?

How much weight do you think customers put on statements from automobile Salespeople? Unfortunately, not much. They still believe, right or wrong, that automobile Salespeople will say anything to make the sale.

So how do you *INSPIRE* them?

By doing everything differently than the competition. But most importantly, by *showing* customers you are different, not just *telling* them you are.

Customers come into dealerships hiding behind defensive shields. If you are honest, professional, and intelligent with them their defenses melt so they become receptive to your sales process.

As you begin to work with your customers think about the fact that three questions are always in the back of their minds:

> ➤ Do I like you?
> ➤ Do I trust you?
> ➤ Do you care about me?

You need to answer these questions for them through what you say and what you do. Your actions, and backing up what you say with follow-up actions, affect customers more than anything you could ever tell them. It instills in them confidence in your professionalism and your integrity. If customers are comfortable with you, the dealership, and the product then they will be *INSPIRED* to buy from you.

Once you've been given the opportunity to *INSPIRE* customers and you've taken advantage of it, only one of two things can happen at the end of your presentation. Either you've done a great job and *INSPIRED* the customer to buy today or you've planted all the right seeds for a return visit. Even if the customer decides to shop other dealerships, which you can assume will happen, you're betting they won't run into a Salesperson as *INSPIRING* as you.

So what happens when customers are on the edge of a decision and call you back asking to meet another Dealer's price? It's a common scenario reported by Salespeople using this concept of *INSPIRATIONAL SELLING*: Customers who've been truly *INSPIRED* are calling back after shopping other dealerships to say they found the car for $ 100 or so less elsewhere, but they liked this dealership, and then they ask them to meet the price. By doing a great job *INSPIRING* customers, customers are now *INSPIRED* to give the Salesperson one last shot at the sale.

So do you do it?

My advice is: Don't match the offer from the other dealership. The reason: You did a better job, as evidenced by the customer calling back, so that extra profit above the other dealership is deserved. Yet, you might split the difference with the customer. The bottom line: You've earned their business and produced a little more revenue than your competition might have.

Remember: The concept is to always *INSPIRE!* Do things differently than the competition, because if you don't, you're going to get caught up in the price war on every customer.

Keep this concept in the back of your mind as you continue through this book and consider how you can be different in each step of the selling process.

5

**Leading
the Customer
Down the Road
to the Sale**

Step #1

The Meet & Greet

"**M**ay I help you?"

It's as old as ancient Romans selling camels in the city square – maybe even older. To many Salespeople meeting and greeting customers is one of the easiest steps in the selling process. After all, they think, "How complicated can it be?"

Truth is, what you say can be very simple, but precisely how you say it must be exacting. Grandma was right: First impressions are important. Don't automatically fall into saying, "May I help you?" just because it's what customers expect. You want to go beyond that so you can *INSPIRE* customers from their very first impression of you.

Remember: When customers enter the dealership their defense mechanisms are at their highest level.

They know the objectives of the game: The Salesperson wants to sell them a car today for as much as possible and they want to take their time and buy it for as little as possible. And customers now, like Salespeople, also know how the game is played. As I said before, customers will do everything they can to get the best price – even lie. They'll also put on a game face that states: I'm in no hurry, I'm willing to shop. I'm willing to wait it out until I find the car I like, the Salesperson I want to do business with, and the price I'm willing to pay.

Your game plan is to start the selling process. But there is plenty of time for that. Your goal in the Meet & Greet is solely to make customers comfortable so they can relax. In your greeting you're only setting a tone for the sales process to come – a tone of mutual trust. We all know how difficult it is to sell somebody a car who has no trust in you and remains defensive throughout the entire process. So you need to avoid statements that cause them to raise their defense mechanisms. To *INSPIRE* customers use statements that make them lower their defenses. You want to make them receptive to you. Rather than meeting customers with any of the high pressure tactics they've encountered elsewhere and have come to expect from the industry, instead you meet them with not only low pressure, but a "negative" pressure, if you will, in order to *draw* them to you. Then you will *INSPIRE* them to do business with you.

When is the best time to start this building of trust?

With the very first impression you give customers: In how you greet them.

There are many different ways for doing the initial Meet & Greet, depending on your part of the country, your dealership, and your personality. Be unique in your greeting, but be sure:

➢ You're enthusiastic.
➢ You smile.
➢ You offer a warm, sincere welcome.
➢ You have a firm, but not Herculean, handshake.
➢ You use Mr. and Mrs. unless they inform you differently.
➢ You use the customers' names often.
➢ You give them time to warm up to you.

Remember: This may be just another sale for you, but for them it's an important day.

For initial greetings my personal favorite is:

> ➤ "Hi. Welcome to the dealership. How may I help you?"

It's cordial, it's simple and to the point, and it's what customers might anticipate, but it's also more. That's my own way of doing the Meet & Greet, but it may not be your way. The best greeting is the one you're most comfortable with, the one that'll put customers at ease, the one closest to your own personality, and the one you'll use.

To start the Meet & Greet off on the right foot introduce yourself, providing your full name, then asking for theirs. For example:

> ➤ "Hi. Welcome to the dealership. My name is David Lewis, and yours?"

This type of introduction should result in a return response with their name. You might even say:

> ➤ "Hi. Welcome to the dealership. My name is David Lewis, and you are Mr....?"

I recommend you call your customers by their last names, as this is guaranteed to never offend anybody, plus will make many of them feel special. If, however, they respond with only their first names I would simply ask:

> ➤ "And your last name is?"

Some highly defensive customers may not want to give you their last name. This doesn't happen often, but it happens. The best response in this case then might be:

> ➤ "Oh, I don't like to call people by their first names without their permission."

And either they'll relax enough to give you their last names or they'll respond with, "First names are fine."

Now, let's look at the next few minutes or so in the sales process. How many times have you heard Salespeople ask something like:

- "Are you buying a car today? If not today, then when?"
- "Is there anybody else that will be involved in the buying decision?"
- "If you're trading in a car, do you have it with you today?"

I'm sure you've heard, or maybe even used, many similar questions.

Not only are customers put more on the defensive by these types of questions, leading them to put up objections, but then many Salespeople meet the objections by trying to defeat them, which only makes customers more defensive. Think about it: Defense mechanisms are reflexive. When attacked physically, people will try to defend themselves without thinking. That's the same thing customers do when you start to probe with questions. You want them to relax during the sales process so you can properly *INSPIRE* them.

Of course, most people know you're going to try and sell them a car today, but there is no purpose served by making it a focal point in the first few minutes of meeting them.

Remember: *INSPIRATIONAL SELLING* is being different from what customers find elsewhere.

Let's see how this applies in a typical situation. Take for example the very common customers' initial defense: "Just looking." This phrase is extremely frustrating to us, especially to a Salesperson in desperate need of a sale. Nobody wants to waste their time with customers who aren't buying today. But remember, studies are very clear and state that approximately 70% of the people that visit your dealership will buy a car within ten to fourteen days. That makes these customers buyers. So why would they make the initial statement that they're just looking?

Customers say this so you won't pressure them. They know the game, a method designed to try to sell them a car today using whatever means possible. Customers are tired of high pressure Salespeople. And the sad part is that high pressure may not be your style at all, but you've been labeled with the rest of us. Customers are merely drawing their line in the sand up-front.

So now we know odds are 70% this particular customer will buy a car in the next ten days to two weeks and they're nervous and scared that you might pressure them into buying a car today.

So how do you handle this situation?

First of all, stop putting the cart before the horse. Don't worry about whether customers are buying a car today, just concentrate on *INSPIRING* them to want to do business with you. Show them how different you are from the rest of the competition.

Odds are they probably made the same "just looking" statement at the other dealerships they visited and probably didn't receive the best of presentations. It could have been no more than a "Help yourself.", a wave of the hand, and a turn of the heel as the Salesperson headed back inside, leaving them to roam the lot alone peering into windows and squinting at price stickers.

So when these customers make it to your dealership you want to:

- ➤ Relax in your approach so they will.
- ➤ Take it as slow as they'd like it.
- ➤ Show them you're not like other dealerships they've visited.

In your pursuit to show them how different you are you'll want to do what the competition does not do. But don't stop there. Do the complete opposite of what customers expect.

For example, my response to customers who initially say they're just looking is:

- ➤ "Great. I'd be happy to spend some time with you showing you the different cars we have. If there's a particular car you like I'd be happy to arrange for you to test drive it. Then I could provide you with a brochure and pricing information to take home and think about it."

Now that is different. I guarantee you there aren't many Salespeople making statements like that.

Let's quickly analyze what I said.

First of all: "I'd be happy to spend some time with you." This lets the customer know they're important to you even if you know they're just looking.

Second, "If there's a particular car you like I'd be happy to arrange for you to test drive it." How many Salespeople want to waste all that time with customers who've said they're not buying today? Not many – unless you want to be different.

Then I stated, "Then I could provide you with a brochure and pricing information..." accompanied by the critical statement, the one customers do not expect, "...so you can take the information home and think about it."

Why in the world would you want to make a statement like "So you can go home and think about it.?"

One reason and one reason only: To lower their defense mechanisms.

Will you try and sell them a car today? Of course you will, but you don't want them to feel that, and certainly not in the initial greeting. You want them to relax and allow you the opportunity to impress them with your product, your dealership, and, of course, yourself.

Now let's consider another frustrating opening statement made by customers: "All I want is your best price on that car over there."

This type of customer is sending you a very clear message. They want to do business, but they know your system and want to have total control. They're afraid that if they let their guard down they're likely to make an impulsive decision they won't be happy with later.

With this customer my response would be:
>   ➤ "Great. I wish more people knew exactly what they wanted. Let's go get the information on the car and then I can give you the best price so you can go home and think about it."

By saying this, you put them at ease.

Again, will you try and sell this person a car today?

Of course you will.

But before any sale can be made, you have to take control of the situation by slowing down the process, and more importantly, reducing the customer's defense mechanisms. Once the customer feels you're not trying to sell them a car today, that you realize they want to go home and think about it, the more they'll relax and allow you to utilize the steps necessary to sell them a car.

Remember: The goal of the Meet & Greet is to carefully start the process of putting the customer in a casual, non-defensive mood.

This can easily be accomplished by simply being different. By letting the customer know that you understand how they feel about the selling process.

Once you've made your opening statement, if the customer appears to be very defensive, then start the process now of releasing those defenses by showing them how different you are.

Now, not every customer needs to be put in a non-defensive mood. Many will follow your process right from the very beginning, so you won't always need to make statements like these. When you get a customer that is very cordial and doesn't appear to be that defensive, casually move on to the next step in the selling process, *INSPIRING* them to buy from you.

Step #2

The Qualification Process

Can this customer afford to buy this car? Or is he
wasting my time?

That's what every Salesperson wants to know as soon
as possible. So they start pounding customers with
questions like:

- "You live near here?"
- "What does your husband do?"
- "Where do you work?" Been there long?"
- "You want to buy, or do you have to lease?"
- "Are you paying cash, or do you need to finance?"
- "Now, on monthly payment, where do you want
  to be?"

It's no wonder customers' defensive shields go up and stay up. It's no wonder they lie. If you begin by asking what price range they can afford it will automatically put them in a situation where they think they might get a better deal by lying. They'll understate their true budget. So what happens? You show them something within the budget they tell you and they're disappointed. A false budget will only entangle the process.

I often ask Dealers: "What if I could work in your dealership for a month and not have any customers lie to me? Would you believe I could do that?" They always express their doubts that it's possible – until I explain it to them.

First of all you have to understand something:
  ➢ Most customers will pay much more than they would initially tell you.
  ➢ What causes them to pay more is their excitement for the product, the Salesperson, and the dealership.
  ➢ The excitement always comes before a decision to pay more.

So you defeat yourself by trying to get information about customers' budgets before they've had a chance to get to know the product, dealership, or you. And, more importantly, you open the door for them to lie to you.

Besides, asking questions pertaining to budget is doing just what every other Salesperson does, and the art of *INSPIRATIONAL SELLING* is to be different. And believe me, if the customer is marginal, you'll find out soon enough.

You see, trying to qualify customers right away is another case of putting the cart before the horse. Actually, you don't need to discuss finances on a car until you find out which car you're talking about.

To ascertain which car they'd be interested in, begin by asking about their desired new car, not about them:
> ➤ "What will the car be used for?"
> ➤ "How often?"
> ➤ "What features and options are on your current vehicle that you'd like on your new one?"
> ➤ "What options aren't on your current car that you'd like on your new one?"
> ➤ And so forth.

You're seeking a very important piece of information. You're trying to find out not only what they'd *like to have* on their new car but more importantly what they *have to have*. The things they have to have are their uncompromising items. Without them there will be no sale.

If a contractor comes in looking for a work truck, you'd be hard-pressed to sell him anything else, right? The customers' essential needs are the main issue at this point, no matter how nonessential they seem to you. Take for example, the retired couple who come in with this criteria: The car must be a good value, of course, but it can't measure any more than 181 inches. Bizarre, right? No, not when you take the time to talk to them, to grasp the situation: The garage in their condo won't take a car any longer than that. By listening, understanding their plight, and working with them, you've gained their trust. Once you've gained their trust, it's just a hop, skip, and a jump to *INSPIRING* them to buy a car from you.

I know what you're saying: Tell me, how do you qualify customers?

You don't. But, by earning their trust so they won't feel compelled to lie to you to protect themselves, believe it or not, they'll qualify themselves.

Your task now is to simply accept that customers will qualify themselves in their own time and proceed with the road to the sale. Once you know their uncompromising criteria, the items they have to have on their new car, you can begin the Inventory Walk & Selection Process.

#3

The Inventory Walk

& Selection Process

Years ago when Salespeople began taking customers on inventory walks it was to present the entire inventory, letting customers walk the lot, hopefully to discover a car that would excite them. However, in the intensity to push up the qualification process, many Salespeople have gotten away from the purpose of an inventory walk: To get them excited about a particular car.

And let's face it: It's so easy to sell a car to someone who's truly excited about it. Just think about the buying frenzies over vehicles such as the 1960's Ford Mustang or Volkswagen Beetle. Customers will buy cars that excite them. Trust them to qualify themselves to do it.

Remember: The selling process is to sell the customer on a car, the dealership, and yourself.

How you move through the Inventory Walk & Selection Process will help in selling the dealership and yourself. If your inventory is scattered and you bounce customers around the lot, then it will hurt you in selling the benefits of your dealership. If you take a very high pressure attitude, forcing the customer into a particular car, it will work against you in selling yourself.

Take your time during the Inventory Walk. If it takes thirty to forty-five minutes to find a car customers like, then so be it. You only get so many opportunities each day, week, and month. If you're too selective choosing which customers you invest quality time with you'll soon find yourself in that eight-to-ten-cars-per-month rut.

Let's go through a typical Inventory Walk & Selection Process.

Let's say you sell Fords and you've greeted a young couple who've come to your dealership looking for a second car. To begin the Inventory Walk let your customers go shopping. Let them stroll down the line of cars, see what they comment on. During this time chat with them about their desired new car.

Once you've established their uncompromising criteria, show them the least expensive car you have that meets it. Start by showing them the Ford Focus. Briefly explain this is the base model, that it comes in a two-door, or four-door. As they look over the car, and its sticker price, you'll see whether this car could be considered. Your only goal at this time is for them to either select or eliminate this particular model.

At this point the customers will do one of two things. Either they will inform you this is not what they want or they'll begin looking at the car.

If they start to take a closer look they will send you some very clear messages. Most will begin by looking at the window sticker. If no comments are made and they continue to look the car over, then you know they accept the price as being within their budget. If they make comments about the price being high, then you might need to move them over to the used car lot.

If they make no comments about price but they don't like the car, this will be very clear and they'll let you know that this vehicle is not for them. Maybe it's too small or just doesn't have the options they'd like. If this is the case then you need to move them up to the next model, the Ford Fusion.

Again, give them time to look the vehicle over. Most will go right for the window sticker and send you the proper signal. If they keep looking the vehicle over then the price is acceptable. Trust customers to send clear messages. If they're still quiet on price, but comment that this car is also too small for their needs and they don't particularly care for it, move them up one more level to the Taurus.

Again they examine the price and look the car over in detail. You offer them the opportunity to sit inside. If it's a car they're excited about very few will refuse. You show them the interior, let them sit inside, point out all the features, share your knowledge of the car. You stop talking from time to time to simply give them the time to experience the vehicle through all their senses and to imagine themselves as owners of the car. They seem genuinely interested in the Taurus. The signals are very clear: They truly like this car. The size is just right, they like the body style, and even though the price is a bit out of their price range they still seem very interested in the car. It's time to move into the Demonstration Ride.

But before we shift to a discussion of the test drive, let's consider a very important issue. What if the customer is enthusiastic about the product but indicates the price is more than they care to spend? Should you continue showing them the Taurus or should you move them back down to the Fusion?

Continue showing them the Taurus. The reason: Nobody wants to buy anything they don't like. So, chances are, even if the price is right on the less expensive model, if they just don't like the car they won't buy it for any price.

Some of you are probably saying to yourself, "Why would I want to continue investing time trying to sell them a car that's out of their price range?"

Because if customers fall in love with a vehicle they'll stretch their budget to fit it. People everyday rearrange their disposable incomes to buy what they like, whether it's dinner, clothes, or even a car.

For example, let's suppose two couples come into your dealership the same day looking for a new car. The Alexanders look at a truck, stating their budget is $500 down and $ 300 a month. The Browns look at a minivan, stating their budget is also $ 500 down and $ 300 a month. When you run the figures for the Alexanders their payment comes in at $ 308 a month. When you calculate it for the Browns it comes in at $ 338 a month. Keep in mind both couples stated they'd like to keep their payment around $ 300 a month. So which couple do you think would be easier to sell a car to: the Alexanders at $ 308 a month or the Browns at $ 338 a month?

You believe the Alexanders would be easier to close, right?

But, now think about it this way: What if the Alexanders feel the truck is O.K., but it's not really the color they want, he'd be happier if it had four-wheel drive, and she wishes it didn't have cloth seats? And what if the Browns think the minivan is just the best family car they've seen, they love all the room for the soccer kids and their stuff, she likes the keyless entry, and he's impressed with its maneuverability? Now which couple would you rather have across from you at your desk?

It's so much easier to close customers on a car they've fallen in love with, even if it might be a bit above their price range, than sell them a car they have no desire for. If they're only lukewarm on a car they'll resist any efforts toward closing.

Sometimes it's difficult to tell when customers are not 100% sold on a vehicle. They may leave the dealership telling you they're going home to think about it, then you never hear from them again. I know it's difficult to understand because as Salespeople we're beaten up every day over price, but price usually isn't the main objection.

Remember: Price is only the objection if your product, dealership, and price are equal to every other dealership they have visited.

If you have done a great job of *INSPIRATIONAL SELLING* and they are impressed by you and your dealership, then perhaps they're just not excited by the car.

If you've successfully guided customers through the Inventory Walk & Selection Process then customers:
  ➢ Have begun to build a sense of trust in you.
  ➢ Have qualified themselves.
  ➢ Have eliminated vehicles not to their liking.
  ➢ Have discovered a vehicle they find enticing.
  ➢ Are ready for a demonstration ride.

Step #4

The Demonstration Ride

Once customers select a car that excites them, one that puts a sparkle in their eyes, it's time to move on to a test drive. There are no magic words of advice to tell you when this moment occurs, other than you'll know it when it comes. They'll send you a signal, either a verbal one or even a visual one, such as that gleam in their eyes. But you'll know when they've found a car that thrills them: They can't wait to drive it.

After you've gotten the keys, start it up and pull it out of the spot so they have more room for opening doors. Then get out and let them get in by themselves. If there's only one person hold the driver's door open so the customer can sit behind the wheel. Two people, let them both get in the front seats. And if there are more, then let them decide who'll sit where. If any of them hesitate, open up the doors and welcome them to sit inside.

Now, let them sit inside the car by themselves for five or six minutes, allowing them on their own to touch, feel, and absorb the excitement of what this new car offers. This might be a good time to go inside for a brochure or some other excuse to let them know you're leaving them alone for a brief period. During this time they'll talk amongst themselves – and this will be a very honest conversation since they're alone.

After sitting in the car by themselves, if they determine this really isn't the right one for them after all, they'll tell you. If so, just keep showing them other cars until they do find one they truly like. However, if this is a car which excites them, you'll know.

After this brief five-minute period you can join them inside the car for the test drive. If there's only one person, then let the customer remain behind the wheel and you get in the passenger side. Two or more people, get in the back seat.

Now take the next ten minutes and fully acquaint them with the inside of this vehicle, making sure they're comfortable in the car. If it's particularly hot or cold, have the driver start the car and turn on the heater or air-conditioner. Cover in detail everything you didn't go over in the Selection Process and briefly recap those you did. You know the product inside and out, now share that knowledge with them. In essence, go through the procedures as if you were actually making the physical delivery of the vehicle to them. Show them how to set the radio, climate controls, and tilt wheel. How to adjust the mirrors, view the instrument gauges, and adjust the seat. Explain every feature on the inside of this vehicle in complete detail.

While you're doing this talking, be careful you don't lose the momentum of the *INSPIRATION* you're creating here. You don't want to fall into the trap of asking any questions that could put customers on the defensive. Your only goal during the Demonstration Ride is to let customers become comfortable with the car, starting the process of acknowledging mental ownership.

Remember: you want them to be so *INSPIRED* they request you take them to the next step in the sales process.

Once you've completed the interior presentation, come right out and ask:

➤ "Would you like to take the car for a drive?"

Not many customers are likely to say "No."

Now is the time to really put into practice being different than other Salespeople customers encounter.

For instance, customers have been told at some dealerships that the Salesperson has to drive the car off the lot, which can isolate a second or third person from the single customer in the front seat with the Salesperson. Surprisingly, then the Salesperson stops only a short distance from the dealership so the customer can drive, creating an awkward "musical chairs" by the side of the road. Many customers have told us they find this stop-and-switch-drivers tactic not only clumsy, but confusing. They're so baffled they spend the next few minutes trying to figure it all out – when they should be concentrating on the car.

But you're different so you do what they don't expect: You let them start out behind the wheel, in control.

Once again, because they've been patterned by other Salespeople, many customers will ask you where you want them to drive. Many Salespeople dictate directions: "Turn right, turn left, turn right at the traffic light. When you get to the stop sign turn right again. At the next stop sign right again and finally one more right-hand turn at the end of the road."

Guess where you are? Right back at the dealership. Total demonstration ride time: Less than ten minutes. Trust me, this is not the way to *INSPIRE* customers.

If customers ask which direction to take as they drive the car out of the dealership, your response should simply be:

> ➤ "Are you familiar with the area? If so, drive wherever you'd like."

If they're new to the area then ask them what type of conditions they'd like to test the car under and then give them some simple directions to roads with those conditions. If you can, you might suggest they drive down a certain street in downtown – one you know that has a stoplight next to a glassfront office building. Then when they pull up alongside the building you can casually comment for them to look at the car reflected in the glass. They'll see a beautiful new car looking like it's right out of a TV ad, with themselves driving it. Most impressive. I've even seen some Dealers who find this tactic so effective they install a large mirror on the side of their building just so customers can see themselves behind the wheel.

During the Demonstration Ride you want to be sure the customers are always comfortable and feel in control. So no matter where they drive, or for how long, you let them.

Now here comes the hard part: Sit back and relax, letting them drive and enjoy. Don't start talking or asking questions.

Why? Because that is the opposite of what they have been led to expect. Also, any time customers spend listening to you now is less time they're thinking about the car and experiencing it through their senses.

If there are two or more people in the car, then just be quiet and wait. Most people cannot have dead silence, so the two will start a conversation. Usually the non-driver will ask all the questions for you: How it rides, accelerates, and handles. The result will be a more honest response. The driver will feel like it's just a normal, relaxing conversation rather than a sales pitch requiring defensive caution. At some point you might ask if they would like to switch drivers if more than one of them will be using the car on a regular basis.

If there's only one person, avoid any conversation pertaining to the car. Talk about the weather, the area, whatever. Let the customer ask you questions if there are any. At the most, within any answers you give, mention the warranty. But stay away from the typical questions that will make the customer think twice about what kind of response to give. Once the customer becomes defensive you start to look just like all the other Salespeople.

Another critical mistake many "old pros" at other dealerships make is not only asking too many questions, but constantly trying to trial close. They'll ask questions like:

- "Can you see yourself owning this car?"
- "Would you like to take it home tonight?"
- "Won't this car look great in your driveway?"

Of course, trial closes turn off customers, putting them on the defensive and leading them to lie. Today there is nothing to be gained by them – and a lot to be lost.

If customers ask when to return to the dealership tell them:

➢ "Whenever you like."

The longer they drive the car the better the chances are of them falling in love with it. Let them take it on the highway, the back roads, or maybe by their house to

see how it parks. But during this whole time the less
you speak, trust me, the better off you'll be in the long
run.

All demonstration drives are different because
customers are different. But, whatever else you do,
don't cut the ride short. Let them drive the car for at
least twenty to thirty minutes.

Now, I bet some of you just said to yourself, "What! A
thirty-minute demo ride?"

Yes, that's right. A twenty- to thirty-minute drive. You
want them to truly fall in love with this car.
Remember: The more they like the car, the dealership,
and you, the easier it will be to sell them.

Also keep in mind: Odds are very slim that other
Salespeople took them on a satisfying, long test drive.

When it's time to return to the dealership let them pull
in and park without comment. Above all, resist the
temptation to make any high pressure, trial close
statements. If you've completed the first three steps
successfully (the Meet & Greet, the Inventory Walk, and
the Demonstration Ride) your customers should be
half way through your *INSPIRATIONAL* sales
presentation. They should be:

> ➤ Very relaxed.
> ➤ Excited about the car they just drove.
> ➤ Ready to have you take them to the next step in the sales process.
> ➤ And starting to realize that you're not any ordinary Salesperson – you're different.

Remember: If you're being different you're on your way to *INSPIRING* them right through to a sale.

Throughout the Demonstration Ride, as in the entire sales process, ask yourself, "What do other Salespeople do in this situation? What do customers expect a Salesperson to do?" Then do the opposite:

> ➤ If other Salespeople dictate the demonstration ride route, you let customers drive wherever they'd like.
> ➤ If other Salespeople ask lots of questions, then keep your mouth shut.
> ➤ If they take their customers on short demonstration rides, then you take them out for lengthy ones.
> ➤ If they ask trial closing questions, you don't.

You want to show your customers how different you are so you can *INSPIRE* them.

Step #5

The Walk Around

After an impressive Demonstration Ride, customers have had time to grow comfortable with the vehicle and with you, and they're reassured that the car which triggered their initial excitement still holds their interest. As you get out of the car, point out features on the exterior of the vehicle while walking around it. Continue to share your knowledge of the car and to build on the *INSPIRATION* you've built up till now.

Your Walk Around presentation is one more way to show customers how unique you are. Take advantage of it. One of the key elements to making yours different is to explain features and benefits of the car that your competition does not. A standard Walk Around presentation covers the basics:

> ➢ Show the space in the back seat and trunk.
> ➢ Show under the hood.
> ➢ Explain all the safety features.

Normal time spent on this presentation, about eight to ten minutes.

You need to do the same, of course, but you'll put forth the extra effort to make it more.

> ➢ First, you want customers to see and realize the rear seat capacity of the car. Have them sit back there, stretch out, and experience exactly how much room is there.
> ➢ Next, open up the trunk, again showing all the available space. Explain in detail about the spare tire, tool kits, and any safety items, like a first aid kit or flares that might come with this particular vehicle.
> ➢ Next, show them all the technology under the hood, giving particulars about the engine size and ease of checking items like oil and transmission fluid.

So how is that any different from what you've been doing all along? Keep in mind the Walk Around is the last opportunity you have to point out to customers the additional values and benefits of the car they've selected and to cement this choice in their minds. So you don't want to breeze over any opportunity to *INSPIRE* them.

Your Walk Around presentation can be different if you elaborate on areas that other Salespeople do not. For example, many safety features, like tempered glass, come on cars today, but few customers understand them and certainly fewer Salespeople take the effort to explain them. If you invest a few minutes telling customers about the safety features on the car they've selected they'll come to one of two conclusions: Either it's unique to this car or other Salespeople weren't aware of it, thus making either the car look more enticing or you look more caring.

Take airbags and ABS brakes, the two most common safety features available. Most Salespeople just casually mention them to customers. If you want to be different, try explaining how they work. The average customer doesn't know and would be impressed.

Ask if they've ever had to apply the brakes hard in rain or snow, how the car started to slide to the right or left, and how their high school driving instructor's words came back to them just in the nick of time: "Pump the brakes! Pump the brakes!" Explain that ABS brakes do the pumping for you, adjusting as much as ten times per second to keep the car from going into a skid and causing a collision.

Then ask if they've ever seen an accident where the driver or passenger went through the windshield. Explain that airbags, used in conjunction with seat belts, save lives. In a collision, within hundredths of a second, airbags deploy, instantly filling the front seat with a large pillow of air which eases the impact on the driver and passenger, keeping them from being projected through the windshield.

Now think of some other safety features and how you might explain them to customers, such as:

> Side-impact, solid steel beams in the doors protecting against side collisions.
> Solid steel beams surrounding the gas tank in case of rear-end collisions.
> Flame retardant cloth blanket installed in the hood, not only to deaden engine noise as most Salespeople think, but also designed to fall on and smother an engine fire.

When you get under the hood you can really *INSPIRE* your customers by explaining the features found in the engine compartment, how each one works and more importantly, how that benefits them. Take, for instance, fuel injection. All vehicles have it now, but most customers don't really understand how it works or what value that has for them. Point out that with fuel injection a computer automatically regulates the amount of fuel so, as they start the car, it will fire up easily without having to pump the accelerator as in past vehicles.

There are hundreds of features on cars today that lend themselves to detailed explanation during the Walk Around. Certainly you won't cover but a few of them. But with each customer select the specific features which would motivate that customer to want to own that vehicle.

Remember: *INSPIRE, INSPIRE, INSPIRE.* Be different from your competition.

At the end of a successful Walk Around both you and your customers are enthused by how well things are going. But be wary of a common trap many impatient Salespeople fall into at this time: Trying to close the deal now. They ask some sort of pre-closing question like: "If we could come together on terms and numbers are you ready to buy this car today?"

All that question can do is drop customers into a defensive position. Most will respond with a sound

"No!," thus deflating the enthusiasm you have built up. By trying to close too quickly you've relinquished all control of the selling process to the customer, who responds with statements like: "You're only the first dealership we've been to." or "All we want at this time is your best price and then we want to go home and think about it."

If a customer does pop up and say, "Yes, I'm ready to buy this car today," it's invariably followed by: "So, what's your best price?" and you're back to square one.

So think about it: Why risk losing all the trust, enthusiasm, and *INSPIRATION* you've built up by sabotaging yourself with a premature close?

However, you do want to know if the customer is interested enough in this particular vehicle to proceed. It would be a waste of time to continue only to find out during the negotiating process that they don't really like the car enough to want to buy it. So you need to ask a question that doesn't jeopardize your credibility, yet keeps you in control of the sales process. It can't put the customer on the defensive, but it needs to provide you with some verification they've selected the right car.

The answer: a simple question like:

> ➢ "Does this car meet all the qualifications and standards you're looking for in your transportation needs?"

Of course, adjust that question to something you feel comfortable with, but be sure the question pertains only to the criteria of the vehicle. Never use touchy words like "buy" or "today." They only scare the customer, making them defensive.

Again, as in the previous steps of the sales process, if customers don't feel this car meets their needs, then head back out to the lot and start the Selection Process from the beginning. If this happens (and it will from time to time, but it's rare) there's no need to get discouraged because this time you're going to go through the process on a foundation of mutual trust.

Customers who are *INSPIRED* and are happy with their selection will now look to you to take them to the next step in the sales process, showing the benefits your dealership has to offer.

Step #6

The Service Walk

This is the point in your sales process where you ultimately answer the question in the back of all customers' minds: "Why should I buy a car from you when I could buy it for the same price down the street?"

You're going to respond by intriguing your customers with how different your dealership's Service Department is. Of course, your dealership has a fine Service Department, with convenient hours and location, reasonable rates, and fine technicians. All dealerships do.

So how do you show customers yours is different?

By presenting it to them. It's that simple, yet it's the step in the sales process that's the most often overlooked by other Salespeople. It's unexpected and it only needs to take about ten minutes or so.

But I bet I know what you're thinking: "Oh my, our Service Department is a greasy mess. Certainly not worth showcasing to customers."

Don't worry about it, customers realize it's the nature of the work that's done there. Besides, when you're walking the customer through your Service Department pointing out benefits to them, they aren't thinking about how dirty the service area might be, they're listening to you. If you're providing them with information that is unique and interesting, they'll be impressed. Impressed with both you and your dealership.

So how do you get them back to the Service Department? The easiest way is with an assumed presentation. Tell your customers you have something interesting you'd like to show them on the way to your office. Then just start walking towards the Service Department. They'll follow you.

Once inside the Service Department, begin to point out the benefits of your dealership's department such as

Saturday hours, loaners, or ten-minute oil changes. Take the opportunity to really show off the department.

Start by orienting them with how the Service Department operates:
  ➢ Where they'll bring the car in.
  ➢ Who they'll speak to.
  ➢ What the procedures are for getting their car serviced.

Next, show them how the service area itself is set-up and how the technicians operate. For example: Explain the approach your department makes toward servicing their car, whether it's a team system where each service writer has a team of three or four technicians working together, or a traditional expert system where each technician is trained and certified as a specialist in one or more areas. Be sure to include the number of years experience your technicians have working on vehicles like theirs, it'll be impressive.

While in the service area, point out some of the new technology available for use on their car such as the computerized system some manufacturers now have allowing technicians to hook the car up to a computer which instantly communicates over phone lines with an engineer's computer at the manufacturer's headquarters. This type of technology is amazing to most customers.

However, if your dealership or manufacturer doesn't have that technology, find some other piece of equipment which you can show your customers, such as the Sun diagnostic machine available at most dealerships, which performs a similar function in that it helps the technician diagnose specific problems.

If your dealership has a Body Shop, by all means, walk them through it, indicating briefly any benefits for them.

Then pass your customers by your Parts Department. Indicate how many parts are available immediately for them, then disclose the retail dollar value of your dealership's parts inventory. Regardless of how much it is, it'll seem like an extraordinary amount of money. Keep in mind the average customer doesn't know what constitutes a small, medium, or large inventory.

If possible, arrange an understanding ahead of time with your Service Manager for him to join you when he sees you with customers on a Service Walk. Introduce him to them, then let him take four or five minutes to cover specific features of the department you haven't. For example, let the Service Manager review the department's hours, how to schedule an appointment, or explain in detail the importance of doing regular maintenance on the car. This brief presentation from your Service Manager will certainly set your dealership apart.

You'll find customers appreciate this short presentation acquainting them with the Service Department. By making them more familiar with all the facets of your dealership – not just the Sales Department – it builds more trust and increases their desire to purchase the car from you and your dealership.

The Service Walk is like passing for the fourth down after you've made three downs with your presentation up till now. So why not go for the down, get your ten yards, and retain possession of the ball?

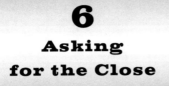

6
**Asking
for the Close**

Once you've completed all the steps to *INSPIRE* customers on the product, the dealership, and yourself it's time to bring them into your office, sit them down with a cup of hot coffee or a cold drink, and begin financial discussions.

In fact, if you've done an effective job of *INSPIRATIONAL SELLING*, your customers will be so *INSPIRED* they'll ask you to lead them through the negotiations. They'll feel relaxed, secure, and trusting, with no need to be defensive or to lie to you. Knowing this, your frame of mind will be very positive as you work to close the deal. There are many ways to go about doing this, and working with your Sales Manager you can decide the best method for you. The following is but one way to complete the road to the sale.

It's time to work from the foundation of trust you've carefully built during your presentation. With this trust, filling out a complete worksheet becomes simple. Keep in mind getting as much information as possible committed to paper begins to cement the sale in the customers' minds. Fill in as much information as you know up to this point, including particulars on the car they've selected.

However, do not write down any prices yet. Again, I repeat, do not write down the price of the car.

While filling in the other information on the car perhaps you can ask them to provide a detail or two (even though you may already know it) just so they'll stay comfortable as you lead into asking them more personal questions. Then you can proceed to complete the remaining blanks on the worksheet, such as their full names, address, and phone numbers for home and work.

Once that's done, customers know what's next and so do you: It's time to present the numbers and ask for the sale.

The best way I've seen to approach the subject of initial numbers is with:

> ➤ "I'll bet you're anxious to find out what your
> investment will be in this car today."

It should bring you a positive response every time.

Call your Sales Manager and ask for the investment for
the car your customers have selected. Call him, don't
go see him. Now is not the time to leave the customers
alone to regroup their game plan.

Your Sales Manager should respond with a full list
price according to your pre-agreed-upon gross in a
payment format. Knowing ahead of time how much,
or how little, gross is necessary will make both of your
jobs simpler. But keep in mind, you've earned the
right to quote full list price, so don't be afraid to ask
for it.

Sure, many of the "old pros" believe in beginning
negotiations by asking customers what price they'd like
to pay for the car. In my opinion, this is a minefield of
ways to hurt the closing process. Giving them the
opportunity to open with a bizarre figure only makes
your job harder. For instance, if they offer $15,000 for
a car that lists for $ 25,000, you're left scrambling to
work them up to a rational figure, with a yawning gap
between you. Unnecessary time and energy are spent
just trying to get them into a reasonable range, often
undoing much of the trust you've worked so hard to

develop. Why put yourself and your customers into a back-and-forth, struggling situation?

O.K., so the "old pros" pry a price out of the customer first, but you don't need to do that. You don't because you've *INSPIRED* your customers through the Selection Process, the Demonstration Ride, the Walk Around, and the Service Walk, and made sure they've fallen in love with the vehicle. So they're comfortable waiting for you to supply them with the price.

Present the numbers to the customer and ask:
   ➢ "Would you like to buy the car?"
Then simply wait for the customer to respond. Of course, you're waiting for them to voice a commitment on their part to the product, the dealership, and you.

Don't undermine this point of commitment by asking any of the common, standard closing questions. For example, don't ask if they're paying cash or getting an auto loan from their bank or credit union. Assume they'll be financing the car through your dealership and quote it to them that way. As we all know, we produce more gross on financed deals. If it's a cash deal they'll tell you. Only then do you provide them with cash pricing.

Remember: How they pay for a vehicle has no bearing on selling the car, the dealership, and you.

As a side bonus of doing it this way, many times customers surprisingly discover your financing is superior to what they'd found elsewhere, which reinforces their positive opinion of the dealership.

Another example of self-sabotage is to tie a trade-in to closing questions. Up till now you haven't brought up a trade because, again, selling the benefits of the car, the dealership, and you, has nothing to do with whether they have a trade or not. But it will have a bearing on the bottom-line and must be considered. So how do you bring a trade into discussion?

By letting customers introduce it. If they have a trade-in, they will tell you now, if they haven't already done so.

When interjecting a trade into the negotiations, don't make the critical mistake many Salespeople make by asking the wrong questions about the trade-in. You only need to know the particulars on the vehicle itself for your appraiser to establish value, such as the year, make, model, mileage, and options, plus if there is any loan payoff. You do not need to know what the customer thinks their car is worth. By doing so you'll only put customers in a defensive position where they feel they need to lie.

Asking customers for the value of their trade is another minefield of ways to hurt the closing process. Either they inflate the value of their trade or they truly believe it's worth more than it is. Letting them commit to this unrealistic figure only solidifies that amount in their minds, sending negotiations off on the wrong track, discouraging everyone. With this unrealistic figure planted in their heads how can a Salesperson then tell them what their trade is really worth?

In practice, Salespeople are so discouraged they don't tell them the truth. Instead, they expend a lot of unnecessary energy persuading their Sales Manager to manipulate the figures, discounting the new car numbers so the trade numbers seem larger. But with *INSPIRED* customers the time and energy are better spent with them, working professionally and steadily toward a close.

Ultimately, asking customers their opinion on the value of their trade will sabotage your profit margin. Let's look at how this works.

For example, if you ask customers what they feel their trade is worth and they reply $5,000, then you return offering only $2,500, wouldn't they be insulted? Most of us would be. So, to save this embarrassment, your Sales Manager dances with the figures, automatically discounting the new car price, showing more for the trade than its appraisal of $ 2,500. Let's say he discounts the car $800, showing the customer $ 3,300 for their trade. Negotiating begins, maybe finalizing the deal with a trade allowance of $3,600 to $4,000, and a discount of $1,100 to $ 1,500.

But what if you do not ask them what they think their trade is worth, simply letting your manager ACV the trade for $2,500. This time you present the numbers to your customers at full list, less the $ 2,500 for their trade. Will they be pleased with the trade allowance of $2,500? Most likely not, resulting in a counteroffer.

But this will be a counteroffer closer to the actual value, perhaps around $4,000, significantly less than the $5,000 they had in their minds. Faced with the ACV given by your appraiser, a professional, they realize a figure of $5,000 is unrealistic, so they adopt a lower number.

In final negotiations you might end up giving the customer between $ 3,000 to $ 3,400 for the trade. However, now you've discounted the new car only $ 500 to $900.

Once you've gotten customers thoroughly committed to purchasing the car they've selected, everyone understands it's just the mechanics of down payments, financing, trade-ins, and negotiation from here on out.

Now, as for how to actually negotiate down to that final number, there are so many ways to handle it that I'm going to leave it up to you. You and your Sales Manager will have your own preferences and can establish your own methods that work best for you.

But I will give you two thoughts to always keep in mind when negotiating price:

> ➢ First of all, don't ever be fearful of asking for the full retail price on your first quote. If you've taken time with the customers, listened to their needs and wants, helped them select a vehicle, given them the benefit of your knowledge of the product, guided them through the complexities of financing, and made the selection process enjoyable for them, then you've earned full gross.
>
> ➢ Secondly, the stronger the presentation you make – the more you *INSPIRE* customers – the greater your odds are of holding more profit. The effort you expend on your presentation will come back to you in profit. Maybe not every

time, but certainly most of the time. So in order to maximize your earnings, you should maximize your presentation. The main lesson here? If you want to make a $3,000 gross, then give a $6,000 presentation.

So, is it possible to sell a car for full list price?

Absolutely! When it comes to gross profit, there's an old saying in the car business: Gross is a state of mind. If you believe you can make lots of gross, then you can. If you believe it's hard to make lots of gross, then you can not.

Keep in mind you've done a professional job of *INSPIRING* the customer during the sales process, so you have earned the right to ask for full list price.

7
Transforming
Objections

Let's suppose you've been working with a young couple buying a new utility vehicle for their growing family. You've taken them through the complete Selection Process – the Demo Ride, the Walk Around, the Service Walk – and you're sure they're in love with the vehicle. He's impressed by this model's performance data over the competition and she really likes all the extra features in the interior, plus they're both happy you have one in red. But you just can't get them to commit to the sale.

You know you gave a dynamite presentation, everything went smooth as glass, and you're so sure you thoroughly *INSPIRED* them. Why won't they commit to the sale? Why are they objecting? Most importantly, how can you transform their objections into agreement, and a sale?

Let's take a look at objections, why customers make them, and how you can turn them around.

There are three main reasons why customers object when asked to buy a product:

> First, they often object impulsively. They don't see the value in the product or they feel the price is not justified.

> Secondly, on a product such as a car they realize there's room to negotiate so they stall, not only putting off having to make a big decision, but also hoping the Salesperson is impatient enough for the sale to lower the price.

> Most commonly, however, they merely fear making a bad decision they have to live with.

Customers' objections pop up throughout the sales process, sometimes even before you can get the customer's name. How do you handle them? Just as in every other part of the sales process, you must do it in an *INSPIRING* way. Be different. Do things and make statements the customer does not expect.

It's safe to say in 99.9% of your sales, the sale will be made when you eventually overcome all your customers' objections. The important thing is for you to be prepared with an immediate response for any customer's objection. The more prepared you are, the more easily you'll be able to handle them. And the more easily you handle objections – with logical and intelligent answers in a calm, professional manner – the more you will *INSPIRE* your customers.

You'll find objections come in one of three types:
1. A refusal to follow your process such as:
   ➤ "I don't need to drive the car."
   ➤ "I'm in a hurry, I just want your best price on..."
   ➤ "How much will you knock off the sticker price?"
   ➤ "I want your best price upfront and I don't haggle."
   ➤ "What's the best interest rate I can get on that car?"
2. A defensive statement such as:
   ➤ "We're just looking."
   ➤ "I'm shopping for the best deal."
   ➤ "This car is already a year old." (looking at a new car when next year's models are already out)
   ➤ "This is a used car." (looking at a demonstrator vehicle)
3. A refusal to purchase such as:
   ➤ "That payment (or price) is too high."

> ➤ "You're not giving me enough for my trade."
> ➤ "I can't afford that payment."
> ➤ "I didn't want to put any money down."
> ➤ "I have that deal beat by..."

How do you respond to objections such as these?

Many Salespeople use pressure to try to transform customers' objections. But that just isn't very effective.

I think you'll all relate to this example. Think back to when you were a teenager, now think about a typical family scene: You wanted to stay out an extra hour at a special Saturday night party. Your parents said, "No. Be home at the usual 11:00." You whined, "Why can't I? All the other kids can." They yelled, "Because we said so!" You tried arguing with them – whining, wheedling, pleading – pressuring them, trying to make them break. They remained steadfast, seemingly stronger with every whine. You ended up running to your room, slamming the door, and vowing you'd never be so hard-hearted with your kids.

Looking back on this scene you can see your parents held their ground because you couldn't give them a valid reason for the extra hour. If they changed their minds without reason, they knew they'd set the stage for more whining, wheedling, and pleading, because you would know it would work. Customers are just like that. They'll hold their ground as long as possible so their minds won't be changed for them by a Salesperson who whines, wheedles, and pleads.

Now think back again to how you felt when your teenage sister asked the following night to stay out an extra hour. When your parents said, "No. Be home at the usual 11:00." she responded with, "I'm confused, Mom. Last week you let me stay at Becky's birthday party till midnight. That was under the understanding you knew where I was, that Becky's parents were there, and that if I was going to be late I'd call. Everything's the same, just the party's at Kathy's." And weren't you jealous when your parents compliantly said she could stay out the extra hour?

Your sister had learned to use logic and reason to overcome your parents' objections. She didn't try to beg, plead, or whine. She reasoned with them. She provided them with logical information which could give them justification for changing their minds.

When trying to counter customers' objections you have to use this same philosophy. Use logic and reasoning to convince your customers to change the way in which they're thinking.

When customers voice an objection the first thing you do is acknowledge their statement and the thinking behind it. This brings down their defenses by showing empathy on your part.

Next, you counter their statement with one of your own in order to balance the scale, offsetting any negatives with positives.

Then you seek their acknowledgement of your statement to push the conversation forward.

Lastly, you close the subject, putting the issue to rest. Of course, in practice sometimes the customer won't let the issue rest and raises another objection. In that case you repeat the same process but on a new track.

For example, let's see how you might respond to one of the most common objections when it comes up early in the process.

OBJECTION:

"I'm shopping for the best deal."

Step one: Acknowledge.

> "Of course you are. As a consumer myself, I would do the same thing."

Step two: Counter.

> "I think you'll find the way we do business here at our dealership refreshing and unique, and it lends itself to that exact consumer philosophy. My management won't even permit me to ask a customer for their business until we've earned the right to do so."

Step three: Seek acknowledgement.

> "And that's the way it should be done, wouldn't you agree?"

Step four: Close.

> "So that's exactly what I'm going to do. Give you logical reasons to do business with us, of which the value and the deal will certainly be some of the reasons."

With this, you have now put this defensive issue at rest, making the customer feel comfortable about moving forward with the process. You haven't attacked their somewhat confrontational statement. Instead you've addressed it with understanding and professionalism, justifying their desire to assure they get a good deal. Of course, you may use entirely different language, but stick to the basic concept.

Some objections, such as this one, are considered "good" because they're easily transformed to a positive. Others are considered "bad" because they're quite logical and are therefore difficult to overcome. So before you can transform them you will need, through suggestion, to lead them into a better objection, one which is easier to overcome. Using an Objection Conversion you change their objection into one which is easier to work with.

Let's take, for example, another common one.

OBJECTION:

"I want to go home and think about it."

Most Salespeople will agree they hear that from at least one out of three customers on their lot. It's tough to respond to such a logical statement. So how do most Salespeople usually reply? With something on the order of:

- "What do you want to think over?
- "Is there anything I missed?"
- "Do you want to take the car home with you overnight?"

And many use any one of the ever-popular "Is it...?" routines:

- "Is it the color?"

- "Is it the payment?"
- "Is it the two-doors?"
- And on and on.

But customers know these common responses so, with their defensive mechanisms kicking in, they're prepared to object again with a statement such as:

➤ "I want to think over if I'm ready to spend all that money."

➤ "No, you did a great job I just don't make snap decisions."

➤ "There's no need to take the car home, just a brochure will be sufficient."

Then the Salespeople react again with another predictable statement and the cycle continues until one of them stops out of sheer, hopeless exhaustion.

The only thing happening here with this impulsive, back-and-forth exchange is that the Salesperson is digging himself deeper and deeper into a hole. Instead you should try to release customers' natural defense mechanisms. Sympathize with what they're saying and let them know you're listening and understand. It will put them at ease.

So how should you respond to the customer objection "I want to go home and think about it.?" If it's early in the sales process a reassuring reply might be:

> ➢ "I understand exactly what you mean. It's a difficult decision to make."

That's all you need to say right now. It starts the process of putting the customer at ease and lowering their defense mechanisms.

However, if you reach the time for the close and they're still objecting, wanting to go home and think it over, it's time to convert this awkward objection to one which is easier to handle.

Remember: Most objections are either a fear of making a bad decision, a stall technique, or an impulsive statement.

So you can, through an Objection Conversion, change the direction of awkward objections by planting the seed for an objection that is easier for you to counter.

In response to "I want to go home and think about it." at the closing table, you might convert the awkward objection by saying:

> ➢ "I understand, it's a difficult decision to make. However, I do find it surprising. Most of my customers are usually pleased to finish the car shopping process once they've found a car that fits their needs and wants, as you said this car does for you. But I'll tell you what I've found. Of the few who do say they still want to think it over,

most are concerned about whether this monthly
payment will fit into their budget. Would you say
you fall into that category as well?"
Since price is the easiest objection to overcome, their
response should be one you'll be able to handle.

Let's take a look now at a few more common customer
objections and how you might handle them. The following
are objections you will normally get while on the lot.

OBJECTION:

"We're just looking."

> "That's great. I'm glad you shared that with
> me. Now I know you don't need to buy a car
> today. I'd be happy to show you all the
> different cars we have in stock, you can test
> drive whichever ones you like, then I can
> provide you with all the literature and pricing
> information you'll need to then go home and
> think about which car best fits your needs."

OBJECTION:

"What are you asking for that vehicle over there?"

> "Certainly. Let me find that out for you right
> away. Let's go and get some information off the

vehicle so I can provide you with the accurate price. And it will give you a quick opportunity to determine if there's any other information you might want to know about the vehicle."

OBJECTION:

"How much of a discount can I get off the sticker price?"

➤ "There is no set amount. It depends on how much of the sticker price is made up of additional factory options. I'll be able to find out the exact amount once we determine exactly which options you want."

If the customer is still persistent you might add something like:

➤ "Our philosophy here is to be more than competitively flexible on that price because we're a volume-oriented retailer. Our management has the means to check competitor's average pricing on a daily basis which guarantees us being very competitive. Once we go inside I'd be happy to get you all the information you need."

OBJECTION:

"I don't need to drive the car. I've already driven one."

Using the Objection Conversion you might say,

> ➤ "Gee, that's surprising. Most of our customers insist on driving the car they have an interest in, even if they've driven them before. But I'll tell you what I've found. Of the few who say they don't want to drive the car, most just feel that by doing so they'd feel more committed to buying the car. They don't want to feel obligated to do so at this time. Would you say you fall into that category as well?"

Following their positive response you then can continue overcoming their objection with:

> ➤ "That's not what we're trying to accomplish. By driving the car you don't have to feel any obligation to make a decision today. We just want to make sure that before you leave to go home and think about this car, that it satisfies all your needs."

OBJECTION:

"I'm shopping for the best deal."

➢ "Well, of course you are. I do the same thing as a consumer myself. I think you'll be pleasantly surprised to know we have a unique approach to doing business here which lends itself to that consumer philosophy. We won't even ask for your business until we've earned the right to do so."

OBJECTION:

"This car is already a year old."
(looking at a new car when next year's models are already out)

or

"This is a used car."
(looking at a demonstrator vehicle).

➢ "I understand exactly why you would feel that way. That's why we certainly take that into consideration on the final pricing. We want to insure you will not pay a penalty for making a smart purchase. You save without sacrificing future value. Let me explain. The primary factor in a vehicle's value is the model year, of course. The next two determining factors are mileage and condition. That's why buying a previous model year or a demo is considered a smart purchase."

OBJECTION:

"I'm intending to shop other dealerships. Whoever gives me the best price is where I'm going to buy the car."

> ➤ "Buying where you get the best deal is not only the smart thing to do, it's the right thing to do. I hope to be able to give you enough information and much more than one reason to allow us to earn your business here. Of course, one of the reasons will be a price that you're comfortable with."

The following are objections you will get while in a closing situation.

OBJECTION:

"Is that your best price?"

> ➤ "At this time that is our best price, but please, understand, there always has to be some flexibility in order to earn your business. All we want is a price that is fair for both you and the dealership. I've never seen management lose a customer's business over fifty or a hundred dollars."

OBJECTION:

"I want to talk to my parents (or friend or advisor) before I make a final decision."

Acknowledge this one with something such as:

> ➤ "It's great you have somebody you have confidence in to help you make these important decisions."

Then continue with:

> ➤ "However, I find it a little surprising you feel the need to talk to someone else since I can tell you really like the car. It's been my experience when customers have felt the need to consult someone, it was usually due to monthly investment considerations. Would you say you fall into that category, too?"

OBJECTION:

"What's the interest rate?"

> ➤ "I really don't know today's rate, but obviously it's important to you. You've probably been to your own bank, what's the rate over there?"

Customers will reply in either of two ways. If they respond with "I can get 8%." you answer:

> ➤ "Gee, that sounds like a great rate, what bank is that with?"

When they respond with their bank name you add:

> ➤ "Again, that's a great rate. And at this part of the process it's going to be your best rate. So why don't we assume you're going to finance the car at your bank."

Then, to change the subject, ask questions pertaining to the vehicle.

If they answer your initial question with "I haven't been to my bank yet." then you ask:

> ➤ "Where do you do your banking?"

When they respond, you add:

> ➤ "You probably have your checking and savings there."

Then wait for their positive response. Follow that with:

> ➤ "At this point in the process let's assume that's where you're going to get your best rate."

Then switch over to a question about the car.

In each instance you have satisfied the customer for the moment, enabling you to continue with the sales process.

OBJECTION:

"That payment is too high."

> ➢ "Thank you for sharing that with me. You probably set up your budget based on a figure that is both affordable and comfortable. But let's take a minute to consider all the savings you'll receive by purchasing a new car. Then you can better determine if this payment fits into your budget or not."

Take this opportunity to show them monthly and yearly savings by calculating and comparing figures from such items as gas mileage, maintenance, repairs, and insurance. When the savings on all of these items are added up, it often offsets the payment enough per month to make it feasible for them.

During negotiations sometimes the approach of calculating savings won't work with objections like:

> ➢ "That payment is too high."
> ➢ "We can't afford that."
> ➢ "This payment is more than I want to spend."

Let's look at how best to handle this difficult objection.

First acknowledge it with:

> ➢ "I understand exactly where you're coming from. Just like you, I try very hard to stay within a certain budget when investing in a large item like an automobile."

Next you want to counter their objection with a positive statement such as:

> ➤ "I'd like to share a thought with you that's always been a concern of mine and maybe yours, too. When purchasing an item I'll be using for years to come, such as a car, I try and think about the future as much as the present. My concern is if I don't invest those few extra dollars today it could come to haunt me in the future. What if each time I drive the car I'm thinking, 'I should've invested a little more to get exactly what I wanted.'?"

As you see, this provides the customer with some thought-provoking concerns yet makes no bold accusations or assumptions. The explanation is in the first person because telling a story of how you or others felt in a similar situation allows customers to listen open-mindedly, then form their own thoughts based on what you have said.

Next you want to take the customers' temperatures and determine if they've bought in to what you just said, so you seek their acknowledgment:

> ➤ "Obviously, the last thing you want to do is make a purchase today that you'd want to change in the future, right?"

Always phrase these questions in a format which provides you with very high odds of getting the response you want. With this example most customers would just agree with a verbal "Sure." or maybe a slight nodding of the head.

Once you've gotten their acknowledgment, then don't be afraid to go for the close. Be direct and to the point:

> ➢ "Keeping that thought in mind, doesn't it make sense to invest those few extra dollars to get exactly what you want? Wouldn't you like to move forward and purchase this particular car?"

If you're continually *INSPIRING* customers, then you're continually earning the right to ask for the sale, so when you are in negotiations, ask for it. So many Salespeople just don't. They're afraid of rejection. But if you have put in the work of *INSPIRATIONAL SELLING*, now is the time to ask for the sale. You may be surprised – many of your customers may be so *INSPIRED* they'll insist they buy the car from you.

8

Managing
Customer
Phone-Ups

You've had your share of "tire-kickers," those daydreamers who come to the lot cruising the new models, maybe wiggling out a test drive, with no intention of ever buying a car. They probably couldn't afford one if they decided to buy it. They're a waste of time. And with experience you learn to weed them out.

But what about the people who call in to a dealership with a question about hours, location, inventory, or most often, price? Do you consider them time-wasting "tire-kickers" too?

You shouldn't. People on the phone, unlike "tire-kickers" who just want to see the cars, have a specific reason to call: They have a valid interest in your product or your dealership. Believe it or not, odds are decidedly in your favor that phone-ups will buy from you. One of the highest percentages of buyers comes from this group. That's why your dealership spends tons of money advertising in the phone book and the newspaper – just so these people will see it and call you.

When you're lucky enough to be on the receiving end of one of these calls into your dealership, take advantage of the opportunity. *INSPIRE* the customer on the other end of the line by being unique and saying the unexpected.

Remember: You are now competing with other dealerships to get the customer to visit you.

Once you've answered calls with a friendly greeting, customers will let you know why they are calling. They may want to know such things as:

➤ "Can you explain the lease in your ad?"
➤ "How much are..."
➤ "Do you have a _____ (specific description) in stock?"
➤ "How much down payment would I need on..."
➤ "What about this rebate I saw on TV?"
➤ "How much is my trade worth?"

If you allow the conversation to take its natural course the one who initiated the call, the customer, will control the discussion, leaving you little room to be *INSPIRING*. So, you want to maintain control throughout the conversation. By doing that you can accomplish four goals:

1. You want to spark the customer's interest. You want to *INSPIRE* them, so act enthusiastic about their call, be professional in how you handle it, and try to use language which makes them feel good.

2. You want to get the customer's name. You should always give your name and then in the course of the conversation ask for theirs. Once they've trusted you with their name, use it!

3. You want to get their phone number. It'll be easier for them if you ask for it at the close of the conversation, after you've built up a rapport with them.

4. You want to get an appointment. When you suggest they come in, don't just say something indecisive like, "I'll be here all day." Instead, show them they're important to you by suggesting a specific date and a firm time for you to meet.

How do you keep focused toward these goals and stay in control of the call?

By being prepared with scripts to handle the most common phone-ups. Let me tell you, if you're not prepared, you'll be dancing on the line, forgetting first one thing then the next, and ultimately, you won't get the appointment.

So let's run through some sample scripts to help you develop your own.

SAMPLE:

"Good morning. This is David Lewis. How can I help you?"

"Do you have a blue, four-door Corolla in stock?"

You respond with:
> ➤ "I'd like to be accurate with that information. Would it be O.K. if I put you on hold for a moment while I check that out for you?"

By putting the customer on hold you have immediately taken control of the call. Now you have to keep it.

When you return to the caller you say:
> ➤ "I'm back. I have that information available and really appreciate your patience. As I said earlier, my name is David Lewis and yours is?"

Now get the customer's full name and then use it!
> ➤ "Ms. Jones, we have a number of those in stock with many different equipment levels, colors, and price ranges. When you come into the

dealership, I would be more than happy to show you the different selections we have. I will then provide you with all the information, literature, and pricing you need to take home and think about it. Would you like to come in today and pick up this information, or would tomorrow be better?"

Then the customer should respond positively which day would be better.

You then select a specific time:
  ➢ "Let me check my schedule. How is 2:15?"
If she seems hesitant about coming in at all, try suggesting another appointment time to soothe her apprehension, and to maintain control.

Once she's committed to a specific appointment, don't stop there. Continue to reassure her with:
  ➢ "Great! Ms. Jones, are you familiar with where we're located?"
If she isn't, read off simple, easy-to-understand directions you've written ahead of time.

Now work to gain her phone number:
  ➢ "If you're going to be late, can I assume you'll give me a call to let me know?"

Certainly she'll respond positively.

Then you reply with:
> ➤ "Obviously, if any changes come up on my end, I'll return the courtesy. And your number is?"

The customer has no problems then giving you the phone number under these circumstances.

Then you confirm the appointment with:
> ➤ "Great! I'll expect you Tuesday at 2:15 here at the dealership. You don't have to ask for me by name, I'll be expecting you. And, Ms. Jones, I'm looking forward to meeting you!"

Then at 2:15 when a woman walks on the lot, you can figure it'll be Ms. Jones and you can welcome her by name.

Now let's look at how to handle a few more common phone-up questions so that you control the conversation. In each instance address their initial question simply, then turn the conversation to your script so you can *INSPIRE* them to make an appointment to come in. But in each case be sure you stress: "...and then you can go home and think about it." This reassures them, allowing you to get their defense mechanisms as low as possible. Of course, be sure to speak slowly, professionally, and with respect.

The beauty of having a script is it'll become second nature to you, so if customers veer from it, you'll be able to return them right to it. You'll also learn how to shape your questions to them so they'll respond with predictable answers.

SAMPLE:

"How much is a new ...?"

> "That model ranges between $ 18,000 and $20,000, depending on the options you select."

Whatever their response, you turn it to:

> "The best thing for us to do is to get together. We can select a vehicle you like, you can take it for a test drive, we can appraise your trade, and then I can provide you with some literature and all the pricing information you need. Then, obviously, you will want to go home and think about it. Would tomorrow morning be good or would in the evening after work be better?"

And you continue to control the conversation throughout the call.

SAMPLE:

"How much would my payment be on that car?"

➢ "That's difficult to answer over the phone as there are so many different options available."

Whatever their response you turn it to:

➢ "The best thing for us to do is to get together. We can select a vehicle you like, you can take it for a test drive, and then I can provide you with some literature and all the pricing information you need. Then, obviously, you will want to go home and think about it. Would tomorrow morning be good or would in the evening after work be better?"

Then continue to control the conversation throughout the call.

SAMPLE:

"How much is my trade worth?"

➢ "Considering all the different factors that go into appraising a vehicle, it would be unfair to you or me to do that over the phone."

Whatever their response, you turn it to:

➢ "The best thing for us to do is to get together. We can select a vehicle you like, you can take it for a test drive, and then I can provide you with some literature and all the pricing information you need. Then we can appraise your trade and, obviously, you will want to go home and think about it. Would tomorrow morning be good or would in the evening after work be better?"

Then you continue to control the conversation throughout the call, working to gain an appointment.

SAMPLE:

"Do you have any in stock with ...?"

> ➤ "Our availability of cars is very large. If it's important to you, then I'm confident we can find a car with that option."

Whatever their response, you turn it to:

> ➤ "The best thing for us to do is to get together. We can select a vehicle you like, you can take it for a test drive, and then I can provide you with some literature and all the pricing information you need. Then, obviously, you will want to go home and think about it. Would tomorrow morning be good or would in the evening after work be better?"

Again, you continue to control the conversation throughout the call, working toward an appointment.

See how it works? In each instance you answer their question as directly as you can, then turn the conversation to take control so you can *INSPIRE* them to come in to see you. Once you have them in front of you, you know you'll be able to deliver a great presentation and *INSPIRE* them to buy from you.

9
Prospecting
New Customers

Did you see the movie "Cadillac Man" starring Robin Williams as an automobile Salesman? In one of the very first scenes he stops to help a funeral director whose hearse breaks down right in the middle of a funeral procession. After the Salesman helps transfer the casket from the hearse to a pickup truck, he offers his card to both the funeral director and the widow. He promises each of them a great deal on a new car. Of course they scold him for being so coldhearted, indecent, and downright sleezy. It's a funny scene. However, the funeral director does show up later to inquire about a new hearse. Funnier still.

But the message from the movie is: This Salesperson was vigilant at prospecting, consistently taking advantage of every opportunity to put his name and profession in front of people. The result: His prospecting works.

Maybe you won't prospect the way "the Cadillac Man" does, but if you want to establish sales in the future, you'll need to do some prospecting. Think about it, prospecting is just what it says it is: Mining today's opportunities for tomorrow's potential sales.

The best place to start your prospecting is with your presentation. Take your time, know your product, be professional, and most of all, be *INSPIRING*. O.K., I know what you're thinking: "Why should I spend one to two hours with a customer on a new car, building value, selling myself and the dealership, when I know I'll probably make only fifty dollars – a whopping thirty-seven bucks after taxes?"

This is not a professional attitude. It's exactly the attitude of a "car salesman," in the business to wrangle a quick buck so they can get on with what they really want to do.

However, professional automobile Salespeople, intending to make a long term career in this industry, look at every customer as a building block to long term income. Look at it this way: Each sale is another deposit in your customer bank. It represents a number of future opportunities for additional sales and higher grosses in the form of repeat sales and referral business. Look at your time in the beginning as career-building years. Sure, some of what you do might not provide gratification and rewards today, but it will tomorrow as you progress in your career.

So, if you're persistent about making *INSPIRING* presentations and using your down times between customers to work at prospecting, you can create a flow of future customers. I know you're saying to yourself: "But prospecting isn't fun. What's more, it's boring, tiresome, and rarely gets results in proportion to the effort."

Sure, it's no fun if you put in endless hours combing the phone book, calling anyone who answers to see if they might be interested in buying a new car. You know, odds are you'll eventually run into somebody who'll listen. Maybe they might even buy, especially if you're sharper than the next Salesperson and come up with a spin on it like calling businesses that need service vehicles. But who wants to invest all that time to maybe sell just one or two extra cars or trucks a year? I know, I know, an extra deal is an extra deal. But is it really worth it?

And, more importantly, what alternatives do you have? You're smart enough to know that to be really successful, you can't depend solely on what walks in the door as a result of your dealership's newspaper display ads.

So can you *INSPIRE* people to contact you first when they're in the market for a new car? Of course you can. By doing, once again, what they don't expect. Market yourself every chance you get, in clever, low-key, unpredictable ways. Be creative, express yourself, and have fun doing it.

Many prospecting opportunities come and go each day and we sometimes overlook the best and most successful ones. For example, let's take a time-worn method of prospecting and reshape it for today's customers. Many Sales Managers often have free Salespeople camp out in the Service Department, schmoozing with the customers, getting them coffee, trying to talk up interest in replacing their exhausted old car with a shiny new one. Or in a variation on this, driving the courtesy van for the Service Department, picking up and delivering customers and talking them up during the ride. After all, these are prospects already in hand, already sold on the value of doing business with your dealership.

Does this work?

Sure, sometimes. But not to the level that would get you excited enough to arrive early in the morning to happily pour coffee or chauffeur people about town.

What would excite you is getting results – customers giving you the opportunity to *INSPIRE* them. Because you're confident that once given the opportunity to *INSPIRE* them, they will buy.

What if you could call each person having their car serviced that day and offer them a new car for less than a $100 per month? Would that spark interest and prompt them to want to speak more with you? Most likely.

Here's how you do it: Go to the Service Department and from the daily service log obtain the names, phone numbers, and vehicle information on each car being serviced that morning. Then, taking no more than a minute's time, establish an estimated ACV based on the car's make, model, year, options, and mileage. Next, using the full list price on a comparable new model, subtract the estimated ACV of their car, resulting in a net figure for a monthly lease payment.

For instance, subtract an estimated ACV of $5,500 from a full list price of $20,000, resulting in $14,500 cap cost to figure the monthly lease payment, with a residual of $12,000, you know the lease payment will probably be under $100. Obviously this lease payment is going to be extremely low because of the cap reduction from the potential trade.

At this point don't worry about the exact ACV, payoffs, or additional options. They'll all be taken into the equation later. Armed with this low figure you now have a rational reason to call the prospect. Tell them you were out in the Service Department and noticed their car being serviced. Noting your dealership is in desperate need for quality used cars, inform them that if they have any interest in upgrading their existing car to a more current model, you've calculated they can upgrade for as little as $X per month. They'll be astonished at how low the payment is.

Now invite them to stop by and see you when they come in to pick up their car. Tell them you have a brochure set aside accompanied by a worksheet with all the figures written down on it. But be careful not to make any comments about buying a car today, or even taking one for a test drive. Your goal at this time is to only get them to stop in and talk to you.

Once you have them in front of you, then you can *INSPIRE* them: Reviewing the brochure, going over the numbers in more detail, and finally offering them a

Demonstration Ride. While explaining the figures on the worksheet, you'll establish the exact ACV for their trade-in as well as any balance owed on it, and adjust the figures accordingly.

Naturally, for this approach to produce sales in any appreciable numbers, like all prospecting, you must be persistent and continue to do it day after day, week after week, month after month. But it will work and it will make you extremely successful.

Look at the numbers involved in just this one type of prospecting: Everyday hundreds of thousands of cars are brought in to be serviced in dealership service centers around the country for warranty work, repairs, and routine maintenance. Most dealerships will service a minimum of ten to fifteen cars per day, with some servicing as many as one-hundred a day. If your dealership services about thirty cars a day and you follow this approach, you should sell an additional fifteen to twenty cars a month. But you must make a long term commitment to it. Don't do it for just a week or two. Do it every day for a couple of months at least and you should see your efforts pay tremendous dividends.

Keep in mind prospecting is solely a numbers game. The more contacts you make, the more people will remember you enough to stop in and speak with you. The more customers you have visit, the more presentations and demonstrations you will make. And the more presentations you make, the more *INSPIRING* you will be and the more cars you will sell.

Another prospecting tactic is to contact potential customers by mail, rather than by phone, and one of the most effective I've seen is a letter of introduction. Why it's so effective is the approach that's used. When customers purchase a car, ask them if they could give you the names and addresses for any friends or neighbors who might be ready for a new car. Reassure them you're only going to send them a letter, not phone them. Show them copies of letters you've sent. You'd be surprised how many customers are so *INSPIRED* and pleased by their car-buying experience that they will be happy to supply you with several. Some Salespeople even offer the customers a little bonus for their help: For every five names, they receive a free oil change.

Each time you obtain names this way you send a letter on dealership stationary which takes the approach of:

Dear Mr. Customer,

This week I had the pleasure of assisting Ms. Sue Client with the purchase of her new 2007 Toyota Camry. She's so excited about it, perhaps she's already shown it to you. I asked her permission to mail her closest friends this letter of introduction in the hope of getting an opportunity to provide you with the same service and pleasant experience I proudly provided Ms. Client.

This will be my only contact. I do not want you to feel uncomfortable or be pestered by phone calls. I'm sure if you'd like my help you will contact me. Just place this letter and business card aside and when you're in the market, please call or come in to see me. I'd appreciate the chance to provide you with the same service.

Thank you in advance.

Sincerely,

Joe Salesperson

Of course you'll phrase yours to suit your own personality and situation, but maintain the same approach.

As a professional Salesperson, when you're prospecting, you're in the unusual position of marketing yourself, not just your dealership or your product. Be sure you always have a professional appearance and a professional attitude toward your customers and your co-workers. This translates into a professional appearance in your car and your office, keeping them neat and clean, with nothing that reflects less than a professional attitude to *INSPIRE* your customers.

For example, you'd like to display on your office wall the award declaring you "Salesman of the Month." A great idea, right? Think again. This could be interpreted by customers as an indication that you are a successful Salesperson because you employ high pressure tactics. Hang the award in your den at home and display photos of your kids and dog instead.

In order to market yourself to potential customers you'll need to put on your creative thinking cap and come up with the best ways for you in your community. Some successful ways I've heard of to reach potential customers include:

> Call any newspaper ads listed under "Autos for Sale." This is someone with changing transportation needs. Perhaps you can help them with the transition.

> Fax a fact sheet on new models to potential business buyers, such as faxing information on

new trucks and vans to landscaping or painting companies.

➤ Check the upcoming lease turn-ins and inquire if you can assist them with a new lease. They'll be needing a new vehicle, whether they lease the same model again, upgrade, or purchase a car.

➤ Wear dealer-logo clothing outside of work, such as a ball cap to your kid's Little League game, or a shirt to a local pub or on the golf course. It's a good ice-breaker for people to start up a conversation with you.

➤ When you frequent a local restaurant with good service, occasionally leave an exorbitantly big tip for your server with a note of thanks written on the back of your business card. Trust me, you'll be remembered.

➤ Register with your local Speaker's Bureau. Offer to give talks to any community group that'll have you. Speak on an auto-related subject, such as the importance of routine car maintenance. Use the opportunity for them to relax and get to know you.

➤ Team up with one of your fellow professionals to organize free how-to seminars targeted to specific groups on specific subjects, such as:

o "Women: Everything You Always Wanted to Know About Cars But Were Afraid to Ask" (with the assistance of a mechanic).

o "How to Squeeze Every Auto Deduction Out of the IRS for Your Business" (with the help of a C.P.A.).

o or "Outrageous Tailgate Partying for Diehard Steelers Fans" (with the help of a local caterer).

No matter what type of prospecting you do – and you'll probably find you'll be using all sorts of tactics – remember to be persistent in doing them. If you find it to be drudgery, then you simply haven't found a method that expresses yourself and brings in the customers for you. Put your creative cap on again and do the unexpected. Then prospect on a scale large enough to achieve a large-scale return on your investment of time. Done competently and consistently, results should come surprisingly soon.

But whatever combination of tactics you use, it is extremely important that you develop a daily plan to put them in action, and stick with it. Your returns will be proportional to your investment.

10
Cultivating
Customer
Follow-Ups

Does this sound familiar? You've just gotten home from a hard day at work. Your feet hurt, you're tired, hungry, and probably a little cranky. You flop down at the dinner table, your muscles start to relax, and just as you put the first bite of spaghetti in your mouth, the phone rings. Thinking it's your teenage daughter out on a date with that strange kid with green hair, you pull yourself up to answer it – only to find out it's someone trying to sell you a cemetery plot or something. Feel like strangling them with the phone line? Of course you do! But then to top it off, just before you hang up on them, they tell you your best friend gave them your number. Now who do you want to strangle?

Feeling this way, knowing this is how it usually plays out, why would you ever follow-up with your customers by asking them for referrals to phone? Just like you, they've had these kinds of calls too many times.

They're not about to release their friends' names and numbers to Salespeople so they can disturb their dinners with useless calls trying to sell them something.

So what other alternatives do you have to asking for referrals to phone, asking if they're in the market for a new car?

There are many, just like with prospecting. O.K., you know you need to expand your scope of contacts. And, yes, prospecting is a necessary part of that. But after that point you need to follow-up on the contacts you've already made. If you don't you've dropped the ball. But what do you do?

You just have to think creatively and apply the principles of *INSPIRATIONAL SELLING*.

When you compile your follow-up list, be sure to include all the contacts you make every week, not just your closed sales. Add in all those people you talked to through your prospecting, whether it was people who registered for a free seminar you gave or someone you met playing golf. Then you can form a plan to follow-up on them.

You have two reasons for following-up with your prospects and customers:

> ➤ First, to guarantee that they'll visit you when they're in the market for their next vehicle.
> ➤ Second, to *INSPIRE* them to send you referrals.

One of the most difficult tasks to accomplish is to *INSPIRE* your customers or prospects enough so they feel comfortable sending their friends, co-workers, and family members to you when they're in the market for a new car. But it can be done.

The strong Salesperson knows how to create a follow-up program that'll accomplish both goals simply by creating the unique persona of a caring Salesperson, someone prospects and customers would want to do business with and would spread that by word-of-mouth. If you conduct your follow-up in a positive and professional manner your customers and prospects will return to you and send more buyers your way than any other form of solicitation. Just consider the ease of selling a return customer another car, or going through the sales process with a person referred by someone you know. It'll be much simpler because the initial foundation of trust has already been built.

As you develop your own follow-up program, keep today's buyer in mind and steer clear of any outdated, clichéd techniques, instead opting for the unexpected. Contacting your follow-ups three to four times a year is often enough to keep your name in front of them, but not so often you become a nuisance.

There are as many ways of following-up floating around out there as there are Salespeople to create them, such as sending birthday cards to your buyers or a card on the anniversary of their purchase. However, customers are so used to them, they are ineffective in today's market.

Another imaginative tactic is to take a minute to photograph the buyers in front of their new car while you're waiting for final papers to be drawn. Then at Christmas send them a calendar with their photo on it. Unlike a generic calendar that might get tossed, they'll keep a calendar with their own photo (and your name) on it all year long.

However, because of your limited time, most of your follow-ups will be by phone, so concentrate on different ways to do it. But remember to always be respectful of the person's time and always have a logical reason for your call. The last thing anyone wants is a useless solicitation call.

Obviously, your most important follow-ups are those to your sold customers. Routinely you call them three days and thirty days after the sale just to see if everything is O.K. with their new car. But what about the next call? What's its purpose?

Some Salespeople are very committed and call their customers every ninety days to check on them and remind them it's time for service. At the same time they then ask for referrals. The problem with this is soon the buyers figure out the true reason for the calls and become very cold and distant, certainly less than *INSPIRED.*

But what if you try this? Ninety days after a sale, call your customers and inform them their car is due for its first lube, oil, and filter change. Let them know you'll be happy to make an appointment for them now over the phone or that they can call back at their convenience to schedule a date and time. Never push them for the appointment. Your sole purpose of this call is a pleasant reminder, nothing more.

Ninety days later it's time for another follow-up call. Again, only remind them it's time for another lube, oil, and filter change. If they're not home and have an answering machine, then just leave a simple message. That's all you need to do. If they've told you they normally do their own oil changes or would rather take the car to a fast lube location for convenience, then that's O.K., too. Still make the call to remind them, they'll appreciate it. Sure, your dealership would like the maintenance done at their Service Department, but your goal is just to show concern that the car is being properly maintained.

Then every ninety days make the same call to the customer. On the yearly anniversary of their purchase you might remind them that next time they're in the dealership having service done they might want to inquire about the yearly check-ups recommended by the manufacturer.

To expand on this principle, try this: Each time you speak with your buyer, work the conversation for a detail you can use to justify the next call. For example, during a call you find out they're planning to drive to Disney World in June. Make a note of that and call them again at the end of May before their vacation, suggesting they bring in their car to have it checked out prior to their trip. Then when you call after the trip to see how the car performed, sometime during the conversation gain the next detail for your file to indicate the time and reason for the next call.

Now, if you do this type of follow-up with every
customer for as long as you're in the automobile
business you'll be successful beyond your wildest
imagination. Just think how many of your customers
will return to you when they're in the market for a new
car. After this much careful attention from you, it
would be hard for them not to at least give you an
opportunity to earn their business again.

Also, if you've done this follow-up successfully, how
could your customer not give your name to any friend,
co-worker, or relative that's looking for a new car?
INSPIRE them during the selling process and *INSPIRE*
them after they've made a purchase and you'll have
more opportunities than you can handle. For
example, one Salesman in the Mid-West using these
methods sold fourteen cars through the referrals from
just one customer.

Would you believe you can take this approach even
further to gain even more referrals? Just repeat this
follow-up concept with every prospect you ever talk to,
whether they buy a car from you or someone else. We
all realize we're not going to sell a car to every person
who visits with us. Some will buy elsewhere and some
will decide to keep their existing car and not buy at all.
But think of the effect it would have on customers if

they shopped with you and then purchased a car from someone else, but you did all the follow-up calls. You called in the first thirty days to check up on their new car, then again every ninety days to remind them to change their oil. Do you think when they're ready for another new car they will contact you? Of course, they will and just think how many friends, co-workers, and relatives they'll mention your calls to.

Many of you are probably saying, "That's ridiculous. I'll be on the phone all day long."

But you really won't. Each call only takes a few minutes and handled in organized groups working from your follow-up list, you'd be surprised just how many you can make in a day's worth of down time. Few dealerships will keep you hopping for more than a few hours out of a normal work day.

Now, what if I told you it's possible to work fewer hours, with less effort, ten to fifteen years from now, and yet still make more money than you're currently earning? Well, people do it every day and so can you. Smart Salespeople realize the effort they put into their career today is an investment in the dividends they'll get back tomorrow. Just think about this: The closing ratios and grosses on repeat and referral customers are double the percentage of common walk-in traffic. So wouldn't it make sense to focus your sales efforts there?

If you concentrate on your residual income – that based on sales to repeat customers and referrals – you'll easily increase your sales income year after year. In order to accomplish that, you'll need to develop a successful follow-up program that works for both you and your customers. Then commit to it and work it consistently every day.

11
Final
Comments

One of the best, but most unseen, benefits of our industry is the opportunity to manage and operate your own business without any risk or investment. For as a Salesperson or Sales Manager you are, in essence, in your own business. A business which has no up-front costs, no expenses, no inventory, no overhead, no payroll, and no risk of failure. You're employed as a partner, and yet carry no risk. You have a tremendous inventory to sell from, free local and national advertising, free phone, and free postage. Your facility, fixtures, and expenses are all covered, and you have a staff to help answer your phone, clean your cars, and service them when they breakdown.

The exciting part is that someone else takes all that risk and in return for your efforts you receive one of the highest profit margins available, as much as 25% of the profit generated – one which most business owners would envy.

Wouldn't you agree being in the automobile business is one of the most rewarding industries in America today? Plus, it provides tremendous room for growth, with over 30% of its members reaching upper management in less than ten years. The potential for financial income is explosive, with most Salespeople reaching the top 10% of income earners in the country.

And as we look to the future there is only an increased level of excitement. The manufacturers are developing some great new cars, Dealers are investing money at an electrifying rate to create newer and more up-to-date facilities, and customers are buying cars at an increasing rate every year. This is creating an urgent need for more Sales Managers, General Sales Managers, General Managers, and ultimately, more Dealers.

To illustrate an important point for the application of *INSPIRATIONAL SELLING* let me leave you with one last little story to think about.

An owner of a sawmill decided to have a contest to see which of his lumberjacks could chop the most timber in a day. The competition for a big bonus and bragging rights as Top Lumberjack got down to the last day and the last two lumberjacks: A six-foot-two, muscle-bound ox of a guy and a five-foot-four, skinny, little runt.   The big guy took one look at his competition and said to himself, "Boy, I've got this contest sewed up. There's no way that shrimp can cut as much timber as I can!"

At 8:00 a.m. sharp the sawmill's whistle blew and the contest began in a flash of axes and a shower of wood chips.   After nearly an hour the big guy stopped chopping just long enough to shoot a glance over at his competition. The little guy was sitting under a tree. The big guy laughed heartily, thinking he'd won. Just then the little guy got up and began swinging his ax again in earnest.   So the big guy began chopping harder, but kept an occasional eye on the little guy. After forty-five minutes he saw the little guy stop again, but on the hour pick up the ax and start chopping once more.   Each hour the little guy did the same thing: He took a fifteen-minute break. The big guy kept chopping, thinking, "He can't last much longer, he has to take fifteen minutes out of every hour to rest. And I'm swinging my ax the whole time!"

When the five o'clock whistle blew, signaling the end of the competition, both lumberjacks put down their axes and waited while the sawmill owner measured how many trees each had cut. When the owner declared the little guy the hands-down winner, the big guy yelled, "How can that be? I don't understand. You took a break every fifteen minutes!"

"Yes," replied the little guy, "Every fifteen minutes I took a break to sharpen my ax."

The moral of this story is: He who has the sharpest ax wins.

So, don't work harder, worker smarter – and take every opportunity to sharpen your ax. Every chance you get, try new ways to expand your horizons and educate yourself.

I hope you find that *INSPIRATIONAL SELLING* can be as helpful to you as it has for so many Salespeople and Sales Managers across the country who have adopted the concept and use it everyday to improve their own business.

They have learned to understand their customers and what makes them buy or not.

They've learned to gain their customers' trust as they lead them down the road to the sale through the Meet and Greet, the Qualification Process, the Inventory Walk and Selection Process, the Demonstration Ride, the Walk Around, and the Service Walk.

They've learned how and when to ask for the close and how to take an approach so they can transform any objections that arise.

They've learned to increase their business amazingly through managing customer phone-ups, prospecting new customers, and cultivating customer follow-ups.

Remember: *INSPIRING* customers works. And works well. In fact, I know of one customer who bought a Mercedes $18,000 out of his price range – it was me.

Like what you read?

Do you want to learn even more secrets from expert David Lewis? He is available to speak to your group.

To schedule a time for a dynamic sales presentation tailored especially to your group and for more information call: 800-374-3314.

INDEX

ORDER FORM

Copy & Mail Order along with a check to:

David Lewis & Associates, Inc.
2116 Sarno Road, Melbourne, FL 32935
          800-374-3314

	quantity	total
Secrets of Inspirational Selling Book $14.95 each		$
Secrets of Inspirational Selling Audio Book on CD $14.95 each		
Florida residents add 7% state sales tax		
Priority Mail shipping & handling		5.00
TOTAL		$

Ship To:

name		
address		
city		zip
phone	phone	

Published in North America
by
David Lewis & Associates, Inc.
2116 Sarno Road, Melbourne, FL 32935